No Country for Black Men

Roger Ball

Fordham University

≡IAP

INFORMATION AGE PUBLISHING, INC.
Charlotte, NC • www.infoagepub.com

Library of Congress Cataloging-in-Publication Data

A CIP record for this book is available from the Library of Congress
http://www.loc.gov

ISBN: 979-8-88730-271-3 (Paperback)
      979-8-88730-272-0 (Hardcover)
      979-8-88730-273-7 (E-Book)

No Country
for Black Men

To my sons
Jonathon Alexander Ball
and
Michael Andrew Ball

Contents

Over the last several years, I have participated in a number of conversations about race, class, socioeconomic status, faith, and politics. I have also been a part of many discussions about the disproportionality of special education designation and suspension rate of Black boys. I have led numerous book club, professional development, and circle conversations on these pressing issues including those with law enforcement. I began to notice patterns. Some White participants remained silent during those conversations which often left the elephant in the room unaddressed. When other facilitators, participants, or I tried to cajole healthy and courageous debates, these individuals often retreated further into their silent and safe cocoons. This was especially true during the pandemic when most meetings took place on Zoom and other online platforms. It was easy for those participants to simply mute their mics, turn off their webcams, and fade into the background. This also took place in general sessions as well as in breakout rooms. They became the "nonparticipating participants." I've had similar experiences at in-person meetings. Such participants would find a cozy spot at the back of the room with like-minded colleagues and engage as little as possible. No amount of protocol including Glenn Singleton's (2014) Four Agreements to (a) stay engaged, (b) speak your truth, (c) experience discomfort, and (d) expect and accept non-closure inspired them to participate in any meaningful way.[1] They left as they came offering nothing and receiving nothing. They remain alienated from the opportunity to grow beyond their established doctrines on race, gender, faith, and socioeconomics.

No Country For Black Men, pages xi–xv
Copyright © 2023 by Information Age Publishing
www.infoagepub.com
xi

During those conversations, others wore rose-colored glasses insisting that racism is dead. They named their Black friends as "proof." They showed pictures of their diverse family that included a Black person who married their sister, brother, cousin, or some other relative. They told stories of being godparents to Black and Brown babies which of course meant that they could never participate in or perpetuate the cycle of racism. And when these arguments fail, they point to the fact that after 400 years, America elected and re-elected a Black president. It's a defense that falls flat every time, but one that is the default argument for many. This group often emote and express what Robin DeAngelo refers to as White fragility and Carol Anderson calls White rage. When confronted by the inequities of society, they experience deep-seated guilt and shame and rage. Those three emotions, once surfaced in any discussion, short-circuit their ability to (a) listen to the experiences, both painful and triumphant, of Black and Brown people and (b) reflect on the power and privilege that they are automatically granted as White Americans. Peggy McIntosh outlines this in clear language in her now classic article, "White Privilege: Unpacking the Invisible Knapsack."[2] Finally, their shame, guilt, and rage prevent them from being vulnerable even when the space is safe because they themselves feel unsafe—unsafe at the prospect that they could be contributors to a world that is unjust for entire segments of the population—and that is too frightening for the ego to endure. Rage and accusation become the currency that is then traded, leaving groups splintered and even more segregated.

Still, during those same conversations, in those same spaces, I have seen many White participants courageously say things like:

- "I am a White person that grew up in a White community that espoused racist values about Black and Brown people. I want to undo what I have been taught through listening, speaking, and doing the work of an anti-racist individual."
- "I don't know what it feels like to be targeted by the police, but I want to hear your experiences."
- "I was that person who was afraid of the Black boy in the classroom, the Black man in the subway, the one who used the N-word in the safety of friends and family."

These participants enrich and inspire conversations that send messages of hope. They enter the space willing to listen, willing to speak their truth, willing to learn, and willing to change. They join in the work of dismantling injustice in all its forms by becoming allies, accomplices, and co-conspirators of the "good trouble" that the late John Lewis spoke about.

In one particular conversation, an elderly Black woman said to me with tears in her eyes, "I want to have these conversations, but only if people are going to be real about the issues that we are dealing with." She continued, "I have been around these parts for a very long time. I know what racism looks and feels like because I have experienced it. I know what segregation and bigotry looks and feels like, because I have experienced them as have my son and grandsons. I don't want to be a part of these conversations if people are not going to be real about the daily threats that Black people, and especially Black men and boys, are facing." She wiped the tears from under the rims of her glasses and pushed through yet another painful story that her son encountered as a younger man. I wrote this book to give voice to those tears.

Within those conversational spaces, my own traumas caused by racism often surfaced in a flood of unexpected emotions. One experience, which you will read about in this book, moves me nearly to tears each time I tell it, whether in casual conversations with colleagues, facilitating professional developments, or leading book clubs. This repeated story and the feelings of sadness that is wedded to it inspired a personal curiosity:

- Why did I feel broken each time I told this story?
- What damages has the experience done to my psyche?
- What was my path of healing (if any) from this traumatic moment?
- What other stories are there that I have buried due to the pain and shame I felt?

This reflective process anchored me to a second experience that did not find its way into this work until now. While this story remained in the forefront of my mind during the two years of writing this book, I couldn't find the words to speak or write about it—until now. After I wrote the conclusion of the last chapter, I met with my amazing editor Jennifer Wyman who said, "Roger, we are almost at the end of this project. It's time you start giving thoughts to your preface, foreword, dedication, and selected bibliography." This invitation to begin putting a bow or final touches on the project caused me to wonder what stories remained untold. This following story came back to me like an old enemy begging to be reconciled.

It was a Saturday, late spring, some years ago. We were busy doing spring cleaning and making room for new furniture. I dropped the seats in our truck and me and my son, Michael, loaded it up with some old furniture to take to the county dumpster located seven minutes from our home. Upon entering the yard, workers pointed out which dumpster to toss the materials in depending on what we had to dispose of. I backed up close to the container and we both worked on throwing things from the truck into the deep empty dumpster. A loud clang echoed across the yard with each piece of dismantled furniture that fell into it. Somewhere along the line, a few pieces of paper might have flown from the truck into the yard. I did not see them, but the worker—a White man—came over once we were done. He pointed across the yard and said, "Those pieces of papers flew out of your truck. You must pick them up because we keep this place clean." Winded from the physical labor that we just completed, both my son and I stood there trying to understand what he was saying. He repeated himself, "When you came here it was clean. Go and pick them up now." My son looked me in the eyes as if to say, "Dad, don't let him speak to you like that." I froze. I said to the worker, "Ok, no problem." I quickly surveyed the open spaces for the supposed papers that flew from my truck. I started picking them up and my son followed.

I felt diminished. This feeling was made worse because my son bore witness to this racism. This wasn't just my experience; it was ours. We got back in the vehicle after searching for and collecting pieces of paper and tossing them in the dumpster and drove back home. We exchanged no words for those seven minutes. I parked the truck in the driveway, and we walked into the house together, never saying a word about what had just taken place. I still wonder if he remembers or experienced the event the way I did.

During the pandemic, I started outlining a book that I wanted to write, a book that I had not read about how Black men and boys are treated in the different spaces in society. I wanted to name my experiences and those of my brothers using clear and raw language. I wanted to shed some light on our plight incorporating stories from my own journey along the way. I wanted to write this book to give voice to my two sons, three brothers, countless male cousins, and all the other Black men and boys in the United States. I wanted for us to find a country we too can call our own.

In Chapter 1, I tell of the challenges that I had as a young immigrant (a theme that lives throughout the book) attempting to find my sea legs in a strange and hostile land. I was intentional in using storytelling not only to give a voice to my experiences but to bring readers closer to the place of suffering. Chapter 2 deals with the wretched ways in which our maleness and sexuality has been demonized. Black masculinity continues to inspire fear and rage in this postmodern world. Chapters 3 and 4 looks at the intersectionality of physical health, mental health, poverty, parity, incarceration, eugenics, and more. Chapter 5 takes a surgical look at our education system that pushes Black boys into special education classrooms, into suspension rooms, and out the door before they are properly educated to compete in a twenty-first century economy. Finally, Chapter 6 names the ways that the Black church has lost its prophetic tradition in confronting racism. The

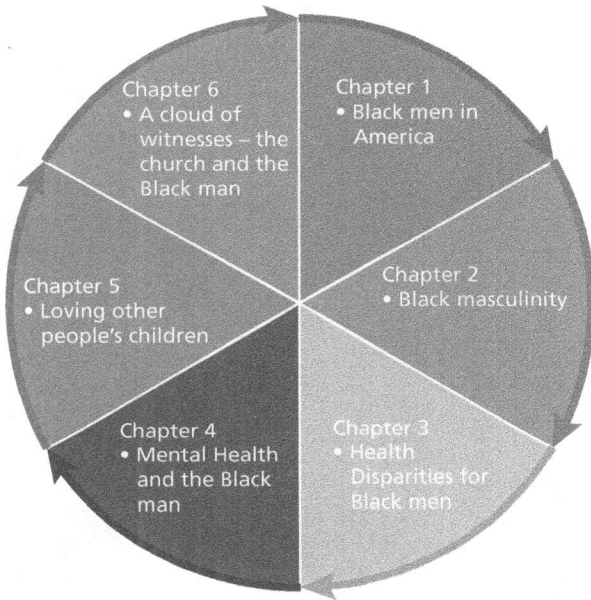

Figure P.1   Visual image of each chapter.

Church is also called to reconversion through rediscovering our tradition of confronting injustice at all levels of society in order to make the world a better place for Black men and our families.

It is my hope that readers will journey with me through the stories, the data, the literature, and their own lived experiences to name and humanize the suffering of Black men and boys in the United States. I hope that we will all become what Donald Capps calls, "Allies of hope."[3]

Notes

1. Singleton, Glenn E. *Courageous conversations about race: A field guide for achieving equity in schools.* Corwin Press, 2014.
2. McIntosh, Peggy. "White privilege: Unpacking the invisible knapsack." (1990).
3. Capps, Donald. *Agents of hope: A pastoral psychology.* Wipf and Stock Publishers, 2001.

1

A Black Man in America

It was 1995. Life was good—no, it was great. I was 19, and high school was almost over. I'd found the love of my life. I was going to be studying social work in college. My future was finally happening. After school and on the weekends, I worked at my future father-in-law's dry-cleaning store on Fulton Ave. in Mount Vernon, NY. I made some good memories there—bonding with my fiancée's dad, cramming for a test in the back room, chatting with customers. Sadly, the building was demolished some years ago. Now, all that remains is an empty lot and the whispers of memories that grow quieter each year. Though, there are a few that yet endure.

One evening in particular stays with me. I had just closed the shop, turned off the machines, killed the lights, pulled the shutters, locked everything down. The light was fading as I made my way to the bus stop to catch the Beeline 60 that would take me back to the Bronx. Boston Road was quiet this time of day. For a few blocks, my only companions were pigeons. I had been studying my shoes, lost in thought, when I looked up and saw that the sidewalk held another—a White woman about 15 yards ahead of me walking, presumably, to the same stop.

No Country For Black Men, pages 1–13
Copyright © 2023 by Information Age Publishing
www.infoagepub.com

I knew the instant she marked me. Her steps came quicker, the grip on her purse tighter. It was obvious she didn't want to let me out of her sight, because she looked over her shoulder every few seconds. I knew what was happening. Anyone with eyes would. In her mind, I was a threat. It was dark, the street mostly deserted, and I was Black.

In that moment, I felt guilty. Guilty for being the source of her fear. I desperately wanted to tell her that I was no threat to her, that I was a good son, a diligent student who was about to graduate high school, an emerging preacher, a young man madly in love with a beautiful woman, Senikha J. Reece. I wanted her to see me as a human being. I imagined myself as a defense lawyer, an advocate or an apologist furiously making the case against whom I was perceived to be—a violent criminal. I was wrong. It was never my job to educate her about her biases.

I slowed my pace to put more distance between her and me. Thus, she got to the bus stop early; I was late. Once there, I held back several yards. I hoped all of this would show her that I would not accost her. I stood there feeling guilty and isolated from my authentic self.

However, guilt soon gave way to anger. I was accused of being something that I was not, a danger to this woman and society. This hurt. It also infuriated me. So lost was I to my frustration and indignation, I didn't notice the bus approaching until it blew past me. I sprinted towards the stop, the woman, and the now open doors she was disappearing behind. With a sinking feeling, I watched those doors close. I knocked on them, but the White bus driver looked at me, then at his left side mirror, and drove away. I stood there in shock, watching the bus disappear in the fading daylight. The next one wouldn't arrive for another hour, about the time it would take me to walk home. I wanted to put distance between myself and the whole painful experience, so I opted not to wait and began the long trek back to the Bronx.

That experience is still with me. The feelings of frustration and sadness linger 25 years later. The memories of victimization are always housed in the mind of the victim, never the victimizer. I am *still* angry at myself. Angry for:

- giving her comfort priority over my need,
- trying to convince her (if only in my mind) that I am not a threat,
- missing the bus after a long day of school and work,
- feeling guilty for something so absurd,
- allowing the experience to inspire suffering a quarter century later, and
- keeping that memory alive for over 25 years.

I took a shower that evening to wash off the shame, frustration, and anger I was feeling. Sleep was slow to claim me as I tossed and turned, trying unsuccessfully to push the experience from my mind. I woke the next morning hoping it was just a bad dream. It wasn't. It was the beginning of the recurring nightmare of what it means to be Black, male, and an immigrant in the United States.

Black and Brown men in the United States feel a sense of disempowerment every day. We have developed survival mechanisms, stepping back to make bigots comfortable. We have bowed our heads low—sometimes so low our necks and backs ache—just to prove that we are harmless, nonaggressive, and humble in the presence of Whiteness. Renowned Harvard scholar and psychiatrist, Chester Pierce, would call my experience at the bus stop "microaggression." The term (however inadequate) describes the relentless slights, shaming, and covert messages that Black and Brown people encounter in our daily interactions with White America. These messages communicate in clear and consistent ways that we are less than, not good enough, dangerous, subhuman, and are undeserving of equal rights and equal treatment under the law.

They tell the Mexican American that he speaks English well "for a Mexican." They tell the Black father who is rushing from work to take his daughter to swimming lessons that his behavior is unusual for men in "this community." I heard the message loud and clear that evening at the bus stop as I watched a White woman scurrying down the sidewalk terrified that, at any moment, I would accost her. It's no wonder Ibram Kendi (2019), author of *How to Be an Antiracist*, detests the term "microaggression."[1] There is nothing "micro" about the daily abuse that one group of people suffers at the hands of another. There was nothing "micro" about my experience that evening. How do I know? Because again, after 25 years, the memory still stings in ways that I do not completely understand. This was not a minor slight or inadvertent infraction. It was a direct assault on my personhood. In "Counseling African American Men: A Contextualized Humanistic Perspective," Phillip Johnson notes, "Historically, the humanity of African American men has been attacked in a cruel and vicious manner. They have been placed outside the human family and often described as beasts or monkeys."[2] One would think that such heinous language is a relic of the past. It's not. Responding to a post about Michelle Obama's eloquence, pediatric anesthesiologist Michelle Herren said, "Doesn't seem to be speaking too eloquent (sic) here, thank god we can't hear her."[3] In the same post, she would go on to say this about the then First Lady of the United States, an accomplished jurist in her own right, "Monkey face and poor ebonic [sic] English!!! There I feel better and I am still not a racist!!! Just calling it like it is."[4]

In July 2016, my wife and I visited Europe, specifically London and Paris. In Paris one evening, we visited the Moulin Rouge Theatre after dinner. While we were in line, the woman in front of me stopped, clearly waiting for someone to join her. Several persons on the line passed her while she waited for her companion. Now, it was my turn to go around her because the line was moving quickly. First, my wife went around her—no problem. As I passed her, she reached out and grabbed my forearm aggressively and said, "You are not allowed to go around me." I stopped and gaped at the woman, shocked by her rudeness and temerity. My wife turned back around only to see this stranger grabbing my hand and yelling that I was not allowed to pass her. Incensed by her behavior, my wife quickly demanded that she release my arm. I, too, chimed in, "Remove your hand from me immediately," I said to her. Her male companion came running up to us, apologizing profusely. Those in front of us turned around to watch and those behind gawked at us openly. The man chided his wife, telling her that her behavior was unacceptable. He then attempted to make small talk about the midwestern state that they were from and in that moment, I thought, "This thing that plagues me in the United States has now followed me to Paris." I had no interest in either his apology or his small talk. I kept looking ahead and mentally renamed the situation as a passing hiccup in order to reclaim the night's narrative as a special moment between my wife and me in the beautiful city of Paris. I refused to allow this small-minded woman to stain this moment, our moment. It is debatable how successful I was at doing so.

White America knows which buzz words will mobilize law enforcement to converge on Black and Brown males with brute and far too often deadly force. Consider the 2020 incident in Central Park NYC between Amy Cooper, a White woman walking her dog without a leash, and Chris Cooper (no relation), a Black man who was bird watching.[5] Mr. Cooper asked her to put the dog on the leash (which, incidentally, is the law). The woman refused and began verbally assaulting him. Cooper began recording her on his cell phone. Not liking this, she proceeded to call 911. Agitated and out of breath, she wails to the dispatcher, "There is an African American man. I am in Central Park. He is recording me and threatening my life and my dog! Please send the cops immediately!"

For persons of color, these words herald an impending assault. "Send the cops" for George Floyd. "Send the cops" for Michael Brown. "Send the cops" for Breonna Taylor. "Send the cops" for Eric Garner. "Send the cops" for my Black and Brown brothers. I am sure that the dispatcher and police officers had no way of knowing that Mr. Cooper was calm, kept his distance from Ms. Cooper, and maintained his composure. Like so many before her, Ms. Cooper eventually found favor with the justice system. Misdemeanor charges against her for falsely accusing Mr. Cooper of threatening her were dropped. This is despite the fact that the event was recorded. There is no country or justice for Black men. Incidents like these continue to cultivate fear for many people of color. White folks can trample on the rights and dignity of others and be exonerated while Black and Brown folks are swiftly arrested and convicted sometimes even when innocent.

This comparative analysis will be made for years to come as historians recast and retell the death of George Floyd, the nationwide protests that followed, and the incredible insurrection that took place on January 6th, 2021. The Black and Brown community will also not forget how law enforcement officers responded to those insurrectionists that threatened their lives by beating them with clubs and makeshift weapons as they breached the Capitol and took over the chambers while members of congress ran for their lives. They will not soon forget how the then president had the U.S. military use tear-gas, rubber bullets, and force against peaceful protesters so that he could get to St. John's Church to pose with a bible in his hand. He told his minions, "We need to dominate the battle space" that was in no way a battle space. Protesting and airing grievances over the death of our sons is not a battle space. The Capitol became that battle space. And on that fateful day when democracy was in the balance, he betrayed the Constitution by encouraging the insurrection. He egged the mob on in an attempt to become a king rather than president whose time in office had expired by the voice and votes of the American people in the middle of a pandemic.

The Risk of Entering the White Space

Many White folks have convinced themselves that race doesn't matter, gender doesn't matter, socioeconomics doesn't matter. Of course, they matter. These are fundamental components of our identity, and, for good or for ill, they are the markers by which society deems us worthy or deficient, justified or undeserving, valuable or parasitic, necessary or expendable. Color blindness "is rooted in the belief that racial group membership and race-based differences should not be taken into account when decisions are made, impressions are formed, and behaviors are enacted."[6] And yet, this happens every day in every sector of society. Color matters when decisions are made about which young man must receive special education. Color matters when decisions are made about which candidate gets hired. Color matters when the police pull over a vehicle. Color matters when the department store manager decides to follow a customer from aisle to aisle to make sure nothing gets stolen. In these cases, it's not just that our color and gender are seen but that decisions are made based on our color and gender. In other words, Black men are targeted for no other reason than because they are Black. These decisions run from the unconscious to the downright dangerous—from a woman holding her purse tightly to a manager in a restaurant asking a Black family to pay for their food before bringing it out. It's dangerous when troopers pull over Black men on the highway. Of course, Black women often have it just as bad if not worse. Mellody Hobson, president of Ariel Investments, a Chicago-based investment firm with $12.4 billion in assets, is the first African American woman to chair the Economic Club of Chicago. She sits on the board of Starbucks and Estee Lauder and served as chair of DreamWorks Animation prior to the sale of the company.[7] She tells of an incident that occurred when she went to a gala in New York with a friend who was running for a seat in the Tennessee State Senate. Upon their arrival, they were quickly shuffled to the worker's room and asked where their uniforms were. The staff assumed that because they were Black, they were workers and not attendees. Suspicion without evidence in such cases becomes a form of neurosis, not of the Black person, but of White folks who draw malicious conclusions based solely on race.

My experience at the bus stop all those years ago—the perception that I was a dangerous, devious miscreant—would, in one way or another, be repeated again and again in my life, at school, at work, on the streets, in supermarkets, restaurants, cinemas, and a hundred other places in a hundred different ways. Just recently, in fact, I was brought face to face with the neurosis of racism. In 2019, my wife and I were invited to an event at a country club out on Long Island. When we got there, we saw that we were among a handful of people who likely would have identified as Black. This was not an unfamiliar situation. Unfortunately, both my wife and I have grown accustomed to operating in "White spaces." Elijah Anderson describes "The White Space" as, "settings in which Black people are typically absent, not expected, or marginalized when present. In turn, Blacks often refer to such settings colloquially as 'the White space—a perceptual category—and they typically approach that space with care."[8] There are profound risks inherent to entering such spaces that White individuals do not face and cannot understand. Anderson is spot on when he says that when Black folks enter White spaces we are always assessing, always looking for kindred spirits. We are always looking to see what other Black individuals are present. We feel profound relief when we see a few Black folks in the audience, at the conference, at the table where decisions are being made. We want to know that we are not alone. There's real comfort in seeing another Black person in the White space, making eye contact, and sending a subtle smile of solidarity. I nodded in Australia the same way I nodded in Greece and in Turkey when I saw a Black couple or family. I see you. You see me.

You might ask, "If you are that uncomfortable in 'the White space' then why even enter it?" I would ask you to imagine how difficult it would be to avoid all such spaces. A Black college student would have a difficult time attending class if he avoided White spaces. He would likely have to drop out of school. (Sadly, that's exactly what many do.) Black businessmen boycotting White spaces would need to turn their backs on Corporate America. Moviegoers would have a woefully short selection of movies from which to choose. The Black woman in labor would have her child at home. You get the idea. The White Space is ubiquitous and unavoidable. In her 2022 confirmation hearing as the first African American woman to the U.S. Supreme Court, Justice Ketanji Brown Jackson, when asked what she would tell young people about their own possibilities of succeeding, not only answered the question but also reflected on her own first semester as a student at Harvard University. She spoke of a lonely and alone night walking through Harvard Yard feeling homesick and out of place in the White space. "I was really questioning; 'Do I belong here? Can I make it in this environment?'" As I watched the hearing, I knew exactly what she felt and meant. The pain came right through the television and into my heart. The feeling that we don't belong comes not from our own sense of inadequacy but from how those spaces are structured. She would go on to say that while on that walk, "a Black woman I did not know was passing me on the sidewalk. She leaned over as I crossed and said, 'persevere.'" We persevere even when we're not welcomed. We persevere even when demeaned and held to a different standard, a double standard. Let's not even discuss how the honorable Ketanji Brown Jackson was treated during those confirmation hearings. I am so glad that she persevered to become the first African American woman to ascend to the Supreme Court.

That country club event is the very definition of a White space. Nevertheless, it was an enjoyable affair. The spread was extravagant. There were serving stations filled with cheeses, crackers, olives, grapes, chicken wings, and so much more. I was at the first station, pondering what tasty morsel I should begin with. Out of nowhere, a White woman appeared, an empty plate in her hands. As she attempted to hand me her garbage, she said, "Can you take these plates and bring me another glass of wine?" And just like that, the risk I knew existed became a reality.

Jolted by the woman's blatant lack of color blindness, I said, with a tinge of annoyance, "I do not work here." The look she gave me was belligerent, unapologetic. "Why did you have to say it like that?" Now she had my full attention. Not only was she blind to her racist actions, she also wanted to dictate my response to her offensive, though unsurprisingly disappointing, actions. By this time, her companion, a White man, joined us, quietly observing. Feeling my ancestral presence and confidence in the White space, I decided to "unnumb" her. Pointing my finger at the guests in the room, I said, "Do you see all these people milling around? Out of everyone here, you chose to take your dirty plate and empty wine glass to me. Why?" I watched the blood drain from her face. I also watched her male companion bow his head to conceal a small grin that said, "You've been made." With righteous indignation, I continued, "You thought that I was a server because I am Black. Admit it. You think the only purpose for Black folks here [in your White space] is to take your dirty plates and serve you." Her mumbled excuse of, "I thought you were one of the servers," reaffirmed my point. She eventually retreated, taking her plates and empty glass back to her seat, her silent male companion at her back. Still, I was glad that another White person was present to bear witness not to me but to his companion.

This is what White privilege looks like. In this White space, it didn't matter that I was an invited guest. I could have been a keynote speaker or the event organizer. I was reduced to the color of my skin and the color of my skin was reduced. Of course, nothing is wrong with working as a server. The issue is not Black servers that were in the White space. The issue is that the White woman's life experience and beliefs told her that a Black person at an event such as this must in some way be subordinate. In her book, *Caste*, Isabel Wilderson makes clear that the United States has done a masterful job of creating a caste system based on race. When we think about caste systems, we think of countries like India. The truth is that for generations people of color have been fighting the caste system that is embedded in the very infrastructure of our society. I will admit that, though I felt confident confronting this White woman, afterwards, I just wanted to go home. I felt pride, anger, and deep sadness. That single experience told me that I did not belong in the White space. It was like being visited by an old, familiar enemy. It was what I felt at the bus stop and in other spaces that I will describe throughout this book. One may name this experience as microaggression, but the very term gives deference to the aggressor. To define such behaviors through the pain and experiences of the person who is being acted against, we probably would imagine terms that echo and correlate to the suffering that so many Black men experience daily by White America. Words like "verbal assault," "degradation," "belittling," "shaming," "violation," "violence-rage" might be more congruent with the pain that is felt by Black men in the White space.

Imposter Syndrome and the White Space

Many years ago, I was a program director for a nonprofit organization serving youth in parochial schools across several boroughs in New York City. In this role, I supervised school social workers and health educators and would therefore visit the schools to observe and provide guidance. One morning, one of my team members and I visited a predominantly White school on Staten Island for the first time. The purpose of that visit was one of observation, feedback, and supervision of my staff that was assigned to the school. My staff member and point of contact at the school, a middle-aged, upper middle class White woman, struggled with how to introduce me to the school staff. It was immediately obvious that she'd not discussed my impending visit to either the school staff or the students. This, despite the fact that all team members were routinely reminded to let stakeholders know when a supervisor would be visiting. The woman introduced me as a "colleague," and I introduced myself as her supervisor and program director. The tension was biting, but I had no intention of diminishing myself to appease those that so cavalierly and comfortably occupy their White spaces cloaked in White privilege.

I have spent much of my adult career in supervisory roles. The elephant in the room has consistently been the palpable unease of middle class, middle-aged White women—women grappling with their own cognitive dissonance about Black men—having to be subordinate to a Black male supervisor. The woman at that school on Staten Island must have felt belittled or diminished having to concede to her White colleagues that her supervisor was a Black man.

My accompanying staff was also White—a tall, blonde-haired, blue-eyed, young woman. We decided to stop at a local pizzeria for lunch before facing the gridlocked traffic back to the Bronx. From the moment we entered that White space, I got the message, loud and clear, that a Black man accompanying a young White woman was not welcome. Evidently, I was unqualified to eat baked dough with tomato sauce and cheese. We endured stares, glares, poor service, and cowardly behavior by small-minded people. When we left, my employee turned to me and asked, "The only reason why we were treated so poorly is because you're Black, isn't it?"

My answer was bald and unambiguous. "Yes." Her eyes welled up with tears, and she attempted to apologize for how I, we, were treated in that White space. I thanked her for bearing witness to what it means to be Black in White spaces but said that if I was undone each time White fragility reared its ugly head, I would become a prisoner to an impotent rage. Ruth Terry, in her *New York Times* article, "How to Be an Active Bystander When You See Racism," reminds us that, "This phenomenon, in which no one in a group of witnesses chooses to disrupt a problematic event" is far too common among people who see and hear racist jokes or comments and fail to respond.[9] This is called "the bystander effect." I certainly did not expect my staff to react in the pizzeria, but the mere fact that she had the courage to name what she saw was encouraging. In her book, *White Fragility,* Robin Diangelo notes, "Most White people have limited information about what racism is and how it works."[10] That day, my colleague, even with her limited understanding, had her eyes and heart open wide enough to bear witness to it.

It's deeply troubling that America is a culture of demented White supremacy that makes people of color feel like imposters in White spaces. My confession here is simply this: I enter all spaces with the spirit of God within me. I enter all spaces on the shoulders of my ancestors. In the words of Maya Angelou, "I come as one but stand as ten thousand."[11] You can't deal with the imposter phenomenon solely on an individual level. It is always easier to diagnose a person rather than the system that has dimmed the light in them. It is always easier to dissect the individual's inadequacies rather than the relentless invasion of messages that tells Black people that they are not and will never be good enough. It's always easier to ask those suffering from this so-called imposter syndrome, "What happened in your childhood that causes you to feel this way?" rather than looking at systemic racism as a root cause. We readily cast this imposter phenomenon as a chink in the individual's armor rather than confronting institutional racism.

Not only are we quick to diagnose, but we also make the racial disconnect our responsibility, dispensing prescriptive solutions to fix our own broken confidence within the White space by:

- looking in the mirror and telling ourselves that we belong,
- over preparing and out-performing everyone, every time because we are in the White space and we will be judged accordingly, and
- engaging in self-talk. "I can do this. I was made for this moment in the White space."

In so many situations, the oppressed are told to adjust to the oppressive regime because the regime is the coin of the realm. There's little conversation about the need to dismantle that which diminishes some and elevates others with no merit other than socially constructed differences of race. Very few create the space for conversation about the disproportionately high number of White folks in positions of power over Black and Brown people in all sectors of society. There is almost no conversation about the lack of diversity among the faculty standing in front of classrooms as instructors to Black and Brown students. I'll have more to say about the need for diversity in education in later chapters.

I am not saying that we should not teach Black and Brown folks the skills and knowledge to survive and thrive in White spaces. I am not saying that we should not remind people of color of our "somebody-ness" in such violent and dehumanizing spaces. But, we must first confront the very construction of those spaces. We must equalize the power structure in a way that anyone can be a supervisor regardless of race, gender, nationality, or disability. We must equalize the power structure in such a way that anyone can be the guest or server without our minds creating binary categories based on superficial differences. When this power structure is equalized, when these racial, economical, and social playing fields are leveled, implicit biases disappear. When this happens, a White woman won't assume that a Black man with several advanced degrees including a PhD could only be there to take her dirty plate and refresh her glass of wine. And what's more, I will be able to refresh my own glass of wine and refill my own plate with crackers, cheese, and succulent olives undisturbed.

Conclusion

James Baldwin opens his book, *The Fire Next Time,* with a letter to his nephew that is both heartwarming and gut wrenching. In it, Baldwin paints a picture about his father and grandfather. He tells him that he looks very much like both men. But, of his grandfather, he writes, "He was defeated long before he died because, at the bottom of his heart, he really believed what White people said about him."[12] The words, "Defeated long before he was dead" crashes down with immeasurable force on my heart creating a deep chasm of sadness. They reveal that his father lost the will to live because he allowed the lies of White supremacy to become his truth. They echo the words of Gregory Ellison, "Cut dead but still alive."[13] Baldwin was brutally honest with his beloved nephew. He goes on to say, "You can only be destroyed by believing that you are really what the White world calls a nigger." I agree with Baldwin. To a point. Though I understand full well why he must exhort his nephew to resist the countless lies told to him about himself. Even when we don't believe or accept the lies about us (subhuman, savage, unintelligent), we are still shaped by their thoughts, attitudes, actions, laws, and policies then as well as now. Baldwin's warning is what most of us men of color must guard against—believing these lies.

My encounters at the bus stop, the country club, the Staten Island school said nothing about the kind of man I am and everything about the character of the women in those stories. I saw their bigotry, not mine. The staff in the pizzeria clued me in to their biases, not my nature, not my character, and certainly not my worth as a human. I have never bought into the lie that because of the shade of my skin, the country of my birth, the zip code I grew up in, or the person that I choose to love that I am less-than, unworthy, deficient. I have always known that I am deeply loved by my family, and that love has served as a shield against this lie. I have always known that I am the youngest of my parents' six children, all of whom continue to love me deeply to this day. In the words of one poet, "Such knowledge is too wonderful for me."[14]

We resist White supremacy, bigotry in all its forms, and we resist imposter syndrome and believing the lies about James Baldwin's father and my grandfather. Toni Morrison was right:

> The very serious function of racism . . . is distraction. It keeps you from doing your work. It keeps you explaining, over and over again, your reason for being. Somebody says you have no language and so you spend 20 years proving that you do. Somebody says your head isn't shaped properly so you have scientists working on the fact that it is. Somebody says that you have no heart so you dredge that up. Somebody says that you have no kingdoms and so you dredge that up. None of that is necessary.[15]

At last, the burden of proving one's humanity does not rest on the subjugated but on the subjugator. We know who we are. We know the artificiality of categorizing and ascribing arbitrary values to humans based on things like hair texture, skin color, gender, sexuality, nationality, zip code, socioeconomics, disability, religion. The only meaning we can ascribe to such variables are the ones we conjure up—meanings which are conjured to elevate some and denigrate others, which are socially constructed to privilege some and exploit others. We have long known that there's no biological basis to race. It is all made up for one purpose, to benefit some and oppress others.

Notes

1. Ibram X. Kendi, *How to Be an Antiracist* (New York, NY: One World, 2019).
2. Johnson, Phillip D. Counseling African American men: A contextualized humanistic perspective." *Counseling and Values 50*(3) (2006): 187–196.
3. University of Colorado Dr. Michelle Herren Calls Michelle Obama "Monkey Face" Says She's Not Racist (Video)—BlackSportsOnline
4. Ibid.

5. "Central Park: Amy Cooper 'made second racist call' against...," BBC, October 14, 2020, https://www.bbc.com/news/world-us-canada-54544443.
6. Evan P. Apfelbaum, Michael I. Norton, and Samuel R. Sommers, "Racial Color Blindness: Emergence, Practice, and Implications," *Current Directions in Psychological Science* 21, no. 3 (2012), 205–209.
7. https://www.actionnewsnow.com/content/national/470497423.html
8. Elijah Anderson, "The White Space," *Sociology of Race and Ethnicity* 1, no. 1 (2015), 10–21.
9. Ruth Terry, "How to Be an Active Bystander When You See Casual Racism," *The New York Times*, October 29, 2020, https://www.nytimes.com/2020/10/29/smarter-living/how-to-be-an-active-bystander-when-you-see-casual-racism.html
10. Robin DiAngelo, *White Fragility: Why It's so Hard for White People to Talk about Racism* (Beacon Press, 2018), p. 100.
11. Angelou, Maya. "Our grandmothers." (1991).
12. James Baldwin, *The Fire Next Time* (Vintage, 2013).
13. G. C. Ellison, *Cut Dead but Still Alive: Caring for African American Young Men* (Abingdon Press, 2013), p. 1.
14. E. Grasham, "Psalm 139," *Interpretation*, 74, no. 3 (2020): 292–294.
15. Toni Morrison, Primus St. John, John Callahan, Susan Callahan, and Lloyd Baker, "Black Studies Center Public Dialogue, Part 2" Portland State University Special Collections, *Oregon Public Speakers* 90 (1975), p. 10.

2

Black Masculinity

In September of 1992, I walked into a new high school overage and under credit. I had just landed at JFK International Airport 3 weeks earlier having left everything behind in Jamaica for a country about which I knew little and about which I never stopped dreaming—America. We came full of hope, my brothers and sisters, grandmother, aunties and uncles, cousins, and I. We came, like so many millions before us, with naught but the belief that America, the land of opportunity, was better than our homeland.

I remember that summer vividly. It was a time of immense change, both for the good and for the annoying. At seventeen years old, I should have had high school in my rear view. In truth, I graduated that very summer from Denbigh Secondary School in Jamaica. But, here I was, starting it all over again (by choice). One weekend in late August, my mom took me to Burlington and Payless for my back-to-school shopping. I was not prepared for the experience that is "shopping" in a land of such wealth and bounty. The clothing my mother bought for me was not secondhand or threadbare. It was new, it was decent quality, and it was abundant. I thought I was kitted out nicely until I walked into one of the classrooms of Evander Childs High

No Country For Black Men, pages 15–28
Copyright © 2023 by Information Age Publishing
www.infoagepub.com
15

School. I don't remember what I was wearing, but almost thirty years later I still remember my Payless sneakers. I remember them because of the teasing that I endured. Steve, one of my new classmates, introduced himself and asked me the brand of my sneakers. The truth was, I didn't know the name because to me, a clean pair of sneakers with no holes in the soles was a win. Who cared what they were called? Nike did not dictate my self-worth. Adidas did not legitimize my place in the world. The microcosm of the American high school? Now that's another story, as I would soon learn. I lifted my foot, found the name, and told him. Well, of course he just wanted to "Payless shame" me by drawing attention to my substandard teen footwear. Predictably, this generated the requisite taunts and jeers commensurate to such gauche fashion choices. I don't remember anyone standing up for me that day. I was confused and embarrassed by the encounter because I never had that experience before. In Jamaica, I wore a uniform to school.

I began that day nervous but excited. I walked home deflated and embarrassed. As I contemplated the shoes on my feet, I thought about how hard my mother worked to make a good life for me and my siblings, the sacrifices she had to make as a single mother living in a foreign, often hostile land. I thought about her living in White American residences as a home health aide for their elderly and infirm, only coming home on weekends to care for us. For years, she spent her weeknights sleeping on sofas. As I replayed Steve's taunts in my head, I admit, for one weak moment, I wondered what I was going to do with the sneakers. What was I going to tell my mother? I loved those sneakers. I wanted to affirm my own self-worth and the sacrifices that my mother was making to put me through school.

The next day, I got dressed, put on the same red and white sneakers, and went to school. This time I did not wait for Steve to find me. I found *him* and asked him if he liked my sneakers. We both burst out laughing. This was my survival mechanism kicking in. One way or another, I was going to assert my claim over my own narrative. Steve and I became good friends after that. Like me, Steve was an immigrant from Jamaica, but he had already been fully indoctrinated into the culture of Black masculinity that was and still is so prevalent among adolescent and adult Black men in this country. That was my first experience in nonconformity. It was also around the time that I started to consider the kind of man I wanted to become.

I did not fit in well with the images of maleness that I saw around me. I didn't follow professional sports. There were no posters of bikini clad women washing sports cars on the walls of my bedroom. I didn't play arcade or video games. I read a lot. I enjoyed learning and spending time serving within my faith community. I was not fashion crazy. I listened to my Jamaican and Caribbean brothers and sisters move between their native tongues and the New York Black slang with ease. I couldn't. So, I didn't. In those early days, I befriended a beautiful young woman in one of my classes. She was from Guyana and had mastered the NY dialect and accent. She told me that she listened to cassettes daily to eliminate her Guyanese accent. I thought that was so strange. It seemed like she was working hard to bury any signs of her nationality, her identity. The pressure to conform often pushes immigrants in the United States to abandon their native language. She eventually told me that she would not date a Jamaican for that same reason. We parted ways shortly thereafter.

From nearly the beginning of my journey in the United States, I tried to stay true to myself and the kind of man that I wanted to become. I was not going to remake myself to fit a cultural norm that did not belong to me nor, more importantly, did I want. Attempting to speak in slang did not feel natural, so I chose not to. Pressuring my mother to get me name brand shoes felt like a betrayal to her sacrifices, so I wore those red and white Payless sneakers until they were barely recognizable as shoes. The next year, mom bought me a pair of Reebok uppers. And you know what? I treated them no differently than I did the Payless pair.

What I did not know as a seventeen-year-old Black boy in New York City was that I was fighting to maintain my individual identity. I did not realize that Steve, my buddy, was an agent of the culture trying to indoctrinate me into how things are in America. I was not buying it.

Doing Black Masculinity

We are all made in the world and by the rules of the world—from the now popular gender reveal parties to how we dress infants in gender specific fashions and colors—from how we react to children when they are in distress to the toys we give them and, yes, to what we tell them they can and cannot do. Christie A. Ford (2011) of Skidmore College wrote a compelling article titled, "Doing Fake Masculinity, Being Real Men: Present and Future Construction of Self among Black College Men." In it, she discusses the connection between Black oppression and the Black man's effort to invent and reinvent himself to reflect more closely what the American psyche expects. Ford asserts that there is a subtle yet fundamental difference between "doing masculinity and being men."[1] Doing masculinity is an affected behavior. It is an inauthentic version of masculinity, a masculinity created, in large part, by White men. Steve, like so many of my brothers, was a victim of this manufactured version of masculinity as much as he was its agent. Ford notes,

Doing black masculinity to signify the process that black college men actively engage in to physically, behaviorally, and materially claim and reclaim a socially constructed, racialized sense of masculinity in black public social spaces, or highly visible sites in which social interactions are likely influenced by societal expectations or group norms.[2]

Every day, the Black man spends an inordinate amount of time contorting his body, clothing, and speech to maintain an image that likely does not reflect his authentic self. It is difficult to quantify the damage this suppression of self does to a person's psyche and spirit. It is exhausting, demoralizing, and dehumanizing.

We brothers are great at keeping each other "in check" when we see someone stepping outside of that socially constructed Black masculinity. As a middle school administrator, I hear and see the subtle and cruel ways that young Black men reinforce Black masculinity group norms. A teen who wears his pants the wrong way is swiftly and brutally castigated. A young man who whips out his Chapstick to soothe his dry, cracked lips is mocked for being "so gay." A kid who hangs out with girls in platonic ways is accused of being one of them. If he works hard at his studies, he is clearly unfit to be a representative of Black masculinity. To this point, Ford notes that failure to adopt a "thuglike image" has serious consequences for men who struggle or refuse to conform. These men are likely to be dubbed (a) homosexual, (b) pretty boys, or (c) sellouts.

"That's So Gay": Black Masculinity and the Accusation of Being Gay

When I was in the second grade attending Old Harbour Primary School in Jamaica, I witnessed something that I will never forget. It was late afternoon, and school had just been dismissed. I can't remember whom I was with, but it was definitely one of my older siblings. There was a big commotion in the streets. People were shouting that a man that was being beaten. A few moments later, the shouting became loud chatter. "Wow, I think he's dead." "The guy was just beat to death." "Someone should call the cops." "Do we just leave him there?" I heard these comments and more. Someone wanted to know who did it. Another wanted a play-by-play. In all this, not one person expressed sorrow for the tragic way this person died, anger over the violence one man wrought on another, distress over the loss of life. No one defended the victim. There was no outrage. Just a detached, vague curiosity, similar to the way drivers rubberneck when they pass an accident.

I heard some saying that he was a "batty man," a derogatory term for a homosexual. My heart quickened as I walked past the scene of the crime.

The details of that dark day have faded. I don't remember what I wore. I can't tell you whose hand I held nor what the weather was like. Yet, I don't think I could ever forget the beaten, bloodied corpse lying in the street. I remember my soul recoiling in horror and sorrow for this man who had no one in his corner—no police, no peacekeeper, no peace maker, no advocate, no one to call for mercy. No justice. He was like the man in Luke's gospel that was beaten, robbed, and left for dead on the road to Damascus. Only this time, there was no good Samaritan to bind his wounds and take him to the hospital. I later learned that the victim was killed for being caught in a homosexual act. My beautiful island had a menacing side to it. In Jamaica, you could be Rastafarian or Catholic, Lutheran or atheist. What you couldn't be was gay.

For many days after that, whenever I closed my eyes, I relived the few moments that I saw firsthand the evil perpetuated by injustice. I heard the shouts and cries, saw the whirling chaos of violence, the bloodied motionless victim, the shock, the disbelief. This stranger showed up in my dreams, his dead eyes filled with censure, bearing down on his murderer, his accusers, and those who saw but did nothing.

I have seen and heard the continuum of responses to our fear of Black men who identify or appear to be gay. I have witnessed the name calling, the taunts and barbs, both in schools and in houses of worship. I have seen the damage left in the wake of such contempt. I have even seen this contempt devolve into murder. This hyper-heterosexual Black male identity has robbed Black men of our authentic selves. Many Black men in the LGBTQ+ community have been forced to hide their sexual identity from this culture of Black machismo. A tragic byproduct of this is the proliferation of HIV in the Black community including women who are in relationships with Black men who are also having sex with other men. Marlon Riggs, in speaking about the experience of Black gay men in America, notes:

> I am a Negro faggot if I believe what movies, TV, and rap music say of me. My life is game for play. Because of my sexuality, I cannot be Black. A strong, proud, "Afrocentric" Black man is resolutely heterosexual, not even bisexual...My sexual difference is considered of no value; indeed it's a testament to weakness, passivity, the absence of real guts-balls. Hence I remain a sissy, punk, faggot. I cannot be a Black gay man because by the tenets of Black macho, Black gay man is a triple negation. I am consigned, by these tenets, to remain a Negro faggot. And as such I am game for play, to be used, joked about, put down, beaten, slapped, and bashed, not just by illiterate

homophobic thugs in the night, but by Black American culture's best and brightest.[3]

Fearful of harsh censure by the church and the Black community, many gay Black men remain closeted. They refuse to identify themselves as gay or even bisexual even though they regularly engage in sex acts with other men. These men have been systematically conditioned to believe in the hyper-heterosexual masculinity of Black men even though they practice differently in the dark. They are brothers on the "down low."

We know that speech has the power to mobilize. It inspires people to act, to march, to take up arms, to do absolute good and unimaginable evil. We need look no further than the insurrection on January 6, 2021 and the words and actions of the outgoing president as he refuses to abdicate the office of the presidency. We also know the power of proclamation from the pulpit. Across the country, millions of people tune in each week to listen to religious leaders anathematize the LGBTQ+ community and its supporters and encourage listeners to take action against them. The Black Church in particular has perfected this art. And yet, as Robert Miller Jr. notes, gay men (and women) are members of our congregations. We preach around them but take and use their gifts to advance our religious missions while rejecting their personhood.[4]

"Stop Acting White": Deviation from the Norm Makes You a Sellout

W. E. B. Du Bois captured the sentiments of Black men and women in America then and now when he wrote, "One ever feels his twoness—an American, a Negro; two souls, two thoughts, two unreconciled strivings; two warring ideals in one dark body, whose dogged strength alone keeps it from being torn asunder."[5] We live by two sets of rules at all times, those imposed by White America and those imposed by Black America. The former reminds us daily that we are not good enough to participate in the American dream. The latter states both explicitly and implicitly that in order to be authentically Black, we must avoid "acting White." There's no country for Black men. I have lost count of the number of conversations I've had with my children about how they are perceived by their peers. They're often told that they are rich, that they act and speak White. This pressure to conform to expected norms has, at times, seeped into our family conversations. A few years back, my then thirteen-year-old daughter said she wished we could move into an apartment building. Her reasoning was that, "All of my Black friends live on the other side of the city in apartment buildings."

In his article, "Slave to the Community Blacks and the Rhetoric of Selling Out," Nigel I. Malcolm notes, "Stigmatization functions to eliminate threats to group cohesion by rhetorically excommunicating heretics." He continues,

> Excommunication denies agency to those labeled "sellout," yet as important it denies agency to other members of the racial group who learn from these negative examples that silence and conformity, rather than freedom of expression and individuality, are to be expected.[6]

In other words, as much as White America reminds us that we are different, Black America reminds itself that it is not White America. Malcolm's use of the term "excommunication" is apt. Black men who do not uphold the Black masculinity standard feel excommunicated by their own community. The teen who likes to read must hide his book from his friends because reading isn't something a Black man does for pleasure. The father who kisses his young son at home avoids doing so in the barber shop where everyone can see. Du Bois had it right; we live double lives in order to adhere to the rules laid out for us by both Americas, the Black and the White.

"Pretty Boy, You Are Messing Up the Image"

A few years ago, I was appointed as assistant principal of a school in the Bronx. One morning, I walked into the building dressed in a suit and tie, my usual workwear. On the way to my office, I was stopped by a teacher who said to me, "Mister, why are you wearing a suit and a bow tie in this building? Do you know where you are? This is the South Bronx, man, this is the South Bronx."

Her words evoked in me the same emotions I experienced when Steve taunted me about my Payless sneakers—hurt, embarrassment, confusion. Guardians of Black masculinity are ready to correct anything—speech, action, dress, and so on—that does not fall within the parameters of acceptable behavior for Black men. Both Steve and my coworker sought to educate me about how a Black man should and should not dress. I'm again reminded of Du Bois; we are forever trapped in two worlds.

Written 100 years after Du Bois's "The Souls of Black Folk," Frank R. Cooper's *Against Bipolar Black Masculinity: Intersectionality, Assimilation Identity Performance, and Hierarchy* illustrates that little has changed. "Popular representations of heterosexual Black men are bipolar. Those images alternate between a "bad" Black man who is a criminal and hyper-sexual and a "good" Black man who distances himself from his Blackness and associates with White norms."[7] Cooper pulls no punches, boldly naming the nature of this duality.

Black men should not be reduced to a trope. They should be free to be their authentic selves without the binary labels of being either Black thugs or wanna be White men. In fact, my sixteen-year-old son wears his bandana, or "silky" as he calls it, his hoodie and, yes, his sagging pants one day and a finely tailored suit and bowtie on another. I would argue that while the outfits are most assuredly different, they are hardly diametrically repellent. White people do this all the time without earning a bipolar label. Why are they exempt from this criticism?

Young men of color need more versions of manhood to emulate. They need to see the Black man who can switch between casual attire and formal attire without losing his individuality or Blackness. They need to see Black men who can do the "cool pose" not just outside of a professional space but also as executives, as teachers, lawyers, doctors, businessmen, community leaders, and religious leaders including pastors and bishops. They need to see the full scope of manhood represented in all spaces where we gather. The Black man who is fluent in slang may also read Shakespeare, Paul Lawrence Dunbar, Du Bois, and Frederick Douglas. Then and only then will we stop equivocating success with Whiteness and criminality with Blackness. We need to see the sagging-pants young father braiding his daughter's hair. We need to see the business executive trading his suit and tie for sweats and sneakers as he heads to the court after work to shoot some hoops with friends he grew up with in the projects. Black men are capable of being both serious and relaxed, professional and casual, tough and sensitive. Maya Angelou wrestled with such contradictions in her poem, *A Brave and Startling Truth*.[8]

> We, this people, on this minuscule and kithless globe
> Who reach daily for the bomb, the blade and the dagger
> Yet who petition in the dark for tokens of peace
> We, this people on this mote of matter
> In whose mouths abide cankerous words
> Which challenge our very existence
> Yet out of those same mouths
> Come songs of such exquisite sweetness
> That the heart falters in its labor
> And the body is quieted into awe
> We, this people, on this small and drifting planet
> Whose hands can strike with such abandon
> That in a twinkling, life is sapped from the living

Yet those same hands can touch with such healing, irresistible tenderness
That the haughty neck is happy to bow
And the proud back is glad to bend
Out of such chaos, of such contradiction
We learn that we are neither devils nor divines

There is much to say about the history of racism in America. There is also much to do about a history that continues to impact the lived experiences and dwarfed economic and social outcomes of people of color. At the same time, the Black community must take a deeper look at how such history has impacted our definition of ourselves and each other. We must disrupt the imposed and the self-imposed accusation of calling success "acting White." We can and we must do better. We need not pressure each other into mediocrity. We need not keep on making each other feel guilty for wanting our rightful piece of the American Dream. Remember the Langston Hughes poem, *I Too Sing America?*[9]

I, too, sing America.
I am the darker brother.
They send me to eat in the kitchen
When company comes,
But I laugh,
And eat well,
And grow strong.
Tomorrow,
I'll be at the table
When company comes.
Nobody'll dare
Say to me,
"Eat in the kitchen,"
Then.
Besides,
They'll see how beautiful I am
And be ashamed—
I, too, am America

Tomorrow must be better than today. Why help a history of prejudice, racism, and discrimination against our people? Why internalize the master's message? To be clear, the idea that education, proper speech, sensitivity, and self-control are traits alien to Black men and inherent to White ones is dangerous to our very survival. In their article, "An Economic Analysis of Acting White," David Austen-Smith and Roland G. Fryer Jr. note, "Many ethnographers argue that peer effects take particularly insidious form: Black peers and communities impose costs on their members who try to 'act white.'" They continue, "Individuals exposed to these social interactions have disincentives to invest in particular behaviors (i.e., education, ballet, proper speech) due to the fact that they may be rejected by their social peer group."[10] The urgency of now that Dr. King spoke about must be realized in how we pressure and police our own cultural and behavioral expectations. What is clear is that Lincoln's Emancipation Proclamation of 1863 that declared, "that all persons held as slaves [within the rebellious states] are, and henceforward shall be free," has not yet been fully realized.[11]

As a people, we must adopt abolitionist thinking that frees us from the belief that White folks hold the monopoly on goodness and kindness, decency and love. We must see Black excellence in our everyday lives. Excellence is always with us even when we choose not to see it.

Hypersexuality and the Larger-Than-Life Penis

America has long been obsessed with the Black man's sexuality and his genitalia. Who hasn't heard that a Black man's penis is...sizable, that his stamina in the bedroom is legendary, his appetite insatiable? His lusts can turn violent. He is prone to rape. Our sexuality and especially our penises have been weaponized. A history of racism and oppression has masterfully linked our very essence with evil. Our skin color? Evil. Our thick lips and flared noses? Evil. Our diction and our slang? Ignorant, un-American, and, you guessed it, evil. Our masculinity and our penises? Evil. What hope do we have of surviving and thriving if our very essence is defined not in human and beautiful terms but in evil and diabolical ones?

History tells us that society fears even the young Black male's penis. On August 24, 1955, fourteen-year-old Emmett Till and his Black friends decided to hang out in the hamlet of Money, a town deep in the heart of the Mississippi Delta. Emmitt's mother sent him to family members while she took a vacation. Emmitt was accused of flirting with the shopkeeper, Carolyn Bryant, who reported the supposed incident to her husband, Roy Bryant, and his brother, J. W. Milam. In the pre-dawn morning four days later, on August 28th, both men showed up at Emmitt's great-grand uncle's home brandishing guns and demanding that Mose Wright hand Emmitt over to them. Mose pleaded with them not to take his grandnephew. In the end, they took him, put him in the back of their truck, and disappeared into the dark. "Bryant and Milam drove to a local cotton gin, forced Till to lift a seventy-four-pound fan in the truck, and drove to the bank of the Tallahatchie River. Milam then shot Till in the back of the head, assisted by his brother in tying the fan around the dead boy's neck, and dropped his body into the river."[12] His family reported the murder to local law enforcement when a White fisherman discovered the mangled body in the river three days later. The killers admitted to taking Emmitt at gunpoint into the night but denied killing him. A trial ensued but both men were found innocent by an all-White jury. Against the recommendation of the local Sheriff, Emmitt's mother had her son's remains returned to Chicago. She further insisted on an open-casket funeral so that the world could see what had been done to her only son. Let all the world see. Let God see what His children did to His son. Let them see that Emmitt carried his 75-pound cross as Jesus carried His cross. Let them see that he was raised from his watery grave 3 days later just as Jesus was raised from the grave 3 days after his crucifixion.

Reflecting on how Black people have been treated throughout history, Toni Morrison (1931–2019), in *The Origin of Others*, notes, "As fascinatingly repulsive as these incidents of violence are, one that is far more revealing than the severity of the punishment is, 'Who are these people?' How hard they work to define Slaves (Blacks) as inhuman, savage, when in fact the definition of inhuman describes overwhelmingly the punisher."[13] She continues, "The urgency of distinguishing between those who belong to the human race and those who are decidedly non-human is so powerful the spotlight turns away and shines not on the object of degradation but on its creator."

Now, I think it's important to point out at this juncture that the Till case is a clear example of he said/she said. Looking at the story with 21st century hindsight, credibility is likely not on Ms. Bryant's side. But, let's assume for a moment that Ms. Bryant's version of events is the truth. There's no utterance, no amount of catcalling, in truth, nothing at all that young boy could have said that justifies the vicious murder of a fourteen-year-old. The egregiousness of Roy Bryant and J. W. Milam's actions are the very definition of extreme overkill. This should never have gone to trial. Even if the events unfolded exactly as Ms. Bryant alleged, what those two men did was unprovoked murder. No one disputed the fact that two grown men shot an unarmed boy to death. What could possibly have been the defense's argument? "Oh, my apologies to the court. I didn't realize the boy whistled and said, 'lookin' good!' That puts things in a new light. Continue with your not-at-all contrived defense." Since when was murder a subjective crime? For as long as the American judicial system was White, evidently.

Roy Bryant and J. W. Milam dragged a child from his bed in the middle of the night, beat him for hours, put a bullet in his head. When he refused to die, they tied a 75-pound fan around his body and buried him in a watery grave. Yet, his dead Black body refused to stay hidden. It cried out in righteous rage demanding justice, demanding the world bear witness to what man wrought against his brother. But, justice would not be done. Not for ten years or twenty or fifty. Emmitt's body has joined the vast sea of Black souls still crying out for justice. But, how can justice ever be done for the atrocities suffered by Black individuals at the hands of White aggressors? Let all the world see. Let them see. Let God Himself see the depravity of His creation.

Predator and Prey: The Proof Is in Our DNA

Black men are accused of being hyper-sexual, sadistic, but our story tells otherwise. The current genetic makeup of African Americans is a testimony to the impact of slavery on Black bodies. If "DNA collection and analysis gives the criminal justice field a powerful tool for convicting the guilty and exonerating the innocent," then we have all the evidence we need to name the sexual predator.[14] In an article titled, "Slavery Changed the DNA of African Americans for All Time," Michael White notes, "Our enslaved ancestors and their descendants mixed with Whites of European ancestry, usually because enslaved Black women were raped and exploited by White men." He continues, "The results also show that essentially all African Americans have some European ancestry as well."[15] Toni Morrison's point is proven here. As much as Black men have been branded as perpetually hypersexual, our DNA says something else. The spotlight of history shines back on the hulls of ships on the high seas fanning out to places like Portugal, Britain, the United States, and the Caribbean. It shines on the hundreds of thousands of Black bodies placed on auction blocks, sold to the highest bidders to work difficult and stubborn fields. It shines on the countless sold to build empires, raise White babies, and buried in unmarked graves.

> The historical record shows that of the 10.7 million enslaved people who disembarked in the Americas (after nearly 2 million others died on the journey), more than 60 percent were men. But the genetic record shows that it was mostly enslaved women who contributed to the present-day gene pool.[16]

There was a time when much of the southern economy was built on forced labor. It's tragically ironic that one of the prevailing stereotypes of the Black man is that he is lazy. The truth is, oppression and systemic racism have locked Black and Brown people into perpetual impoverishment. This has been conveniently interpreted as laziness. Our sexuality has been maligned, but our DNA tells a far more compelling and violent story about predator and prey.

Conclusion

The wonder of White supremacy is its seemingly impenetrable sustainability. Even today, White America is *still* ignorant of the carnage it continues to wreak on Black and Brown people. White people are so entrenched in their privilege they are unable to imagine a world where a Black man is the victim of unprovoked White aggression. Black men are rapists. Black men are violent. Not White men. Never White men. America watched the lynching of George Floyd. Saw it happen right in our living rooms. Saw a White man murder a Black man. And yet, Derek Chauvin's guilt was questioned by more than a few, enough that he thought he could convince a jury of his innocence. We. Saw. Him. Murder. A. Man. This is not something open to debate. It is not a matter of opinion. It's a devastating reality that, in White America, it *is* a matter of opinion because in White America, skin color is a component of righteousness.

John Blake of CNN said, "There is nothing more frightening in America today than an angry White man." He continues, "It is not the 'radical Islamic terrorist' . . . nor is it the Brown immigrant or the fiery Black Lives Matter protester or whatever the latest bogeyman is that some politicians tell me I should dread."[17] Blake might be factually correct, but no number of facts can recast White men for what they have done and continue to do. They have enslaved continents, annihilated tribes, pillaged lands, raped nations, banned indigenous tongues, banished native religion while ramming a European Christ down the throats of millions. And after all that carnage, they sit at their mahogany desks and write a history of the world where they are the heroes and indigenous peoples are the evil barbarians, where their conquests are God-sanctioned and righteousness belongs to the White man. They boarded ships and found new worlds that were already populated with God's children. In the name of Kings and God, they laid claim to those lands dividing them up among themselves. In the words of Christopher Columbus, "I discovered many islands inhabited by numerous people. I took possession of all of them for our most fortunate King by making public proclamation and unfurling his standard, no one making any resistance."[18]

Notes

1. Kristie A. Ford, "Doing Fake Masculinity, Being Real Men: Present and Future Constructions of Self Among Black College Men." *Symbolic Interaction* 34, no. 1 (2011), 38–62.
2. Ibid., 42.
3. Marlon T. Riggs, "Black Macho Revisited: Reflections of a SNAP! Queen," *Black American Literature Forum* 25, no. 2 (1991), 393.

4. Robert L. Miller Jr., "Legacy Denied: African American Gay Men, AIDS, and the Black Church." *Social Work* 52, no. 1 (2007), 51–61.
5. W. E. B. Du Bois, *The Souls of Black Folk* (New York, NY: Signet Classic, 1969), 45.
6. Nigel I. Malcolm, "Slaves to the Community: Blacks and the Rhetoric of 'Selling Out,'" *Journal of African American Studies* 19, no. 2 (2015), 120–134.
7. Frank Rudy Cooper, "Against Bipolar Black Masculinity: Intersectionality, Assimilation, Identity Performance, and Hierarchy," *UC Davis L. Rev.* 39 (2005), 853.
8. Mays Angelou, *A Brave and Startling Truth* (New York, NY: Random House, 1995).
9. Clinton, Catherine. *I, too, sing America: Three centuries of African-American poetry.* Houghton Mifflin Harcourt, 1998, p. 9.
10. David Austen-Smith and Roland G. Fryer Jr., "An Economic Analysis of 'Acting White,'" *The Quarterly Journal of Economics* 120, no. 2 (2005), 551–583.
11. Abraham Lincoln, "Emancipation Proclamation, January 1, 1863," National Archives 6 (2015).
12. Anne Sarah Rubin, "Reflections on the Death of Emmett Till," *Southern Cultures* 2, no. 1 (1995), 45–46.
13. Toni Morrison, *The Origin of Others* (Harvard University Press, 2017).
14. National Institute of Justice, "DNA Evidence Basics," August 8, 2012, https://nij.ojp.gov/topics/articles/dna-evidence-basics
15. Michael White, "How Slavery Changed the DNA of African Americans." *Pacific Standard* (psmag.com)
16. Kenneally, C. "Large DNA study traces violent history of American slavery." *The New York Times* (2020).
17. John Blake, "There's Nothing More Frightening in America Today than an Angry White Man," CNN, November 21, 2021, https://www.cnn.com/2021/11/20/us/angry-white-men-trials-blake-cec/index.html
18. Mackenzie Ash and Laura Sherman, "World History: The West and the World," (2014), p. 24.

3

Cut Dead and Barely Alive

The Health Disparity

By oppression and judgment, he was taken away. Yet who of his
generation protested? For he was cut off from the land of the living;
for the transgression of my people, he was punished.
—Isaiah 53:8

In the United States, Black males have a higher mortality rate than any other demographic. This is true for both Black boys and Black men. We are the last to be employed and the first to be fired. The first to be kicked out of school and the last to graduate (if at all). We are incarcerated younger and receive longer sentences for lesser offenses. We're the least likely to be paroled and have the highest rate of recidivism. The Hebrew prophet Isaiah foretold of the suffering that Jesus Christ would experience at the hands of the secular government and His religious contemporaries. A modern rendering of the ancient poem becomes an ode to Black men. Through systemic oppression, we are painted as subhuman, violent, and monolithic thus barring us from opportunities that are readily available to others and keeping the American Dream beyond our reach. Black men exist on the

No Country For Black Men, pages 29–43
Copyright © 2023 by Information Age Publishing
www.infoagepub.com
29

margins of the U.S. Constitution, on the borders of academic success. We have to work twice as hard as our White counterparts only to be paid less and promoted last, if at all.

The worst part of this tragic reality is that such data points are not hidden, buried in some dusty, forgotten tome. No, they're in plain sight, yet the world remains blind to them. Still, there's been not a lick of righteous indignation or effort to redress inequality in any serious way either locally or nationally. Such disparities are accepted as part of the sociopolitical landscape, unfortunate byproducts of American capitalism. The Black man's place in the American caste system has, since even before its founding in 1776, always been at the bottom. Maybe because of this, it has become a potency woven into the very fabric of our country as though God Almighty deemed it thus and is therefore sacrosanct. But, as Cassius said to Brutus, "The fault my dear Brutus is not in our stars, but in ourselves." There is nothing natural about the caste system in the United States. It has been constructed socially, politically, and economically and must be dismantled with all deliberate speed.

No Country: Health Care and the Black Body

In 1972, Jean Heller, an investigative journalist and writer, lifted the curtain on a government-sanctioned, racial medical study perpetrated against African American men.[1] "In 1932, the U.S. Public Health Service (USPHS) initiated an experiment in Macon County, Alabama, to determine the natural course of untreated, latent syphilis in Black males. The test comprised 400 syphilitic men, as well as 200 uninfected men who served as controls."[2] Penicillin, the drug used to treat the disease, was withheld from participants. In 1969, the Center for Disease Control saw no reason to discontinue the study. For forty years, this barbaric, dehumanizing study continued unchecked, wreaking untold devastation on these men and their families. For forty years, no one cried out for mercy, no one said this was wrong. It wasn't until 1972 that Jean Heller blew the lid off the whole thing. By then, of the 400 Black men subjected to this barbarism, only seventy-four were still alive. It is thought that upwards of 100 of these men—my brothers—died as a direct result of the progression of syphilis. And, while these men suffered, the cure was readily available to White men. It took a journalist to point out that this was morally and ethically wrong. The doctors conducting the study were perpetrating a crime against humanity. More, they were breaking the oath they took when they became doctors. In fact, they violated it so fully it begs the question of whether they were even listening to the words they spoke when they became doctors: "I will prevent disease whenever I can, for prevention is preferable to cure. I will remember that I remain a member of society, with special obligations to all my fellow human beings, those sound of mind and body as well as the infirm."[3]

Pseudo-outrage then followed. Panels were convened to determine whether the USPHS study should continue, its moral ambiguity intact, or halted due to what should have been doctrine: No individual should be denied appropriate medical care—in this case, a course of penicillin—full stop. No one. One panel concluded that the study was "ethically unjustified," language that sounds rather anemic and almost reluctant. It certainly doesn't encapsulate the suffering Black men endured at the hands of White scientists; though, truly, no words can best express injustice the magnitude of which these men experienced. Even the post-intervention language sounds numb, unaffected, and distant from the place of the crime. What is it that causes White people to go to such extreme measures to punish people that do not look like them?

Today, we wonder why Black men are suspicious of doctors. We call it stubbornness and machismo without considering the historical facts. The Black community has never forgotten the Tuskegee Syphilis Study. In their article, "Raising the Ivory Tower: The Production of Knowledge and Distrust of Medicine among African Americans," Jason Wasserman and his colleagues point out several historical truths African Americans faced at the hands of the medical community:[4]

- Slaves were forced to use medicine they were not familiar with.
- African Americans had limited access to care, and any care they did get was inadequate.
- They were punished for practicing African medicine to treat injury and illness.

The medical community faced scrutiny during the height of the HIV/AIDS epidemic. Conspiracy-like conjecture arose about the "real cause" of the proliferation of HIV on the continent of Africa and the diaspora. James Jones summarized it thus:

> Above all, many Black Americans saw AIDS through the prism of race, which brought more than three and a half centuries of White–Black relations into focus. Slavery, sharecropping, peonage, lynching, Jim Crow laws, disfranchisement, residential segregation, and job discrimination were the substance to which many African Americans reduced all American history, forming a saga of hatred, exploitation and abuse.[5]

When COVID-19 struck the world nearly forty years later, the medical community was again subject to censure. While the government pulled out all the stops to get everyone vaccinated, while they rolled out commercials, enlisted community leaders to be the messengers of just how safe the COVID-19 vaccines are, they forgot the root cause of the suspicions in the first place. They forget that Black folks were proven right about the Tuskegee study. They forget that Black folks were proven right about the fact we have been treated like lab rats. What does it mean for the Black community to struggle to get quality healthcare only to have free and immediate access to the vaccine? Black communities had among the highest infection rates, severe illness, and death from COVID-19. They also saw the greatest economic devastation—all because of preexisting vulnerabilities and inequities that were compounded by this dreadful virus. Here are 10 strategies the CDC used to encourage Black people to take the COVID-19 vaccine:

1. *Vaccine Ambassadors.* Vaccinated individuals were empowered to talk to their own communities about the benefits of getting the vaccine.
2. *Medical Provider Vaccine Standardization.* Community physicians who might have had preexisting relationships with patients were invited to provide the vaccine as a standard of care.
3. *Medical Reminders.* Patients were bombarded with messages about upcoming appointments, reminders, recommendations, walk-ins, and so on, to increase the vaccination rate.
4. *Motivational Interviewing.* This is a long-established approach that falls under the theory of changing application to change attitude, belief, and behaviors. This means first understanding the patient's level of hesitancy and its causes and then providing information to reduce such hesitation.
5. *Financial Incentives.* At the height of the pandemic, you couldn't turn on the radio or TV without hearing some shiny incentive to encourage vaccination. These ranged from lotto tickets to gift cards to cash awards and more. There was an ever-expansive partnership between private and public institutions to create financial incentives to increase Black and Brown communities' participation in the vaccine program.
6. *School-Located Vaccination Programs.* Moving vaccinations inside the school building dramatically increased participation. Faith and other community organizations were often included in this effort. This approach attempted to answer the question of equity. It brings the resource to the community where families live, work, and play. Black families would benefit more from this approach not just with vaccinations but with other service deliveries as well. Again, many are suspicious of the herculean effort to make the vaccine available to all

members of the community. This level of access to healthcare is not something many are familiar with, thus the suspicion and distrust.

7. *Home-Delivered Vaccinations.* While many professionals have historically been reluctant to go into "those communities," in this instance, the medical community was pushing into not only communities of color but also into our homes to deliver the vaccine. Some were grateful for the convenience; others were gravely suspicious of such herculean efforts to administer vaccines.

8. *Workplace Vaccination Programs.* Similar to the process employed in schools, mobile trucks and offices converted into vaccine sites allowed members of the workforce to conveniently obtain their vaccinations on the job. Those who chose to get it elsewhere were given paid time to get vaccinated. Additionally, in some cases, days off were granted for those suffering side-effects from the vaccine. This was unprecedented. In many cases, people didn't have to present insurance cards in order to access care.

9. *Vaccination Requirements.* This strategy, while effective in maximizing compliance, also served as a powerful statement for the Black community. The message in many public institutions and in the private sector was clear: "Get vaccinated by this date, or you will be terminated." Many in the Christian community saw this as a sign of end-of-days. Other Christian conservatives (both White and Black) saw this as the Mark of the Beast—a biblical reference to a time when Christians will be persecuted for believing in Christ. Accepting the mark will be the coin of the realm to purchase, sell, or conduct any sort of business. For those who ascribe to such belief, the vaccine fit the bill. Such requirement and resistance by those in the community caused job loss and financial distress. For many, this was simply another lever of control.

10. *Effective Messages Delivered by Trusted Messengers.* In rolling out these strategies to increase vaccinations, politicians were the least trusted messengers. Though, during the height of the pandemic, Governor Cuomo took the spotlight as the nation's most effective and trusted communicator in managing resources, information, and the pandemic itself. His weekly broadcast was engaging, transparent, and, above all, informative. He was trusted and effective, so much so that his approach became a model for the rest of the country. However, Cuomo was the sole exception. Scientists and doctors were said to be most dependable. Though, this has not necessarily been true for the Black community. For us, the clergy has been considered to be especially trustworthy. In fact, during the pandemic, I was invited to sit on the Governor's Task Force. We provided guidance

and messaging on how best to reach our communities to increase vaccination.

Ask many Americans to speculate about the reasons for the health disparities among men of color and you quickly get responses that shine the spotlight on us. Our parents are accused of shepherding us inadequately, our "culture of violence" in NYC and Chicago are employed as a central pillar of our health disparities. Our "poor work ethic, welfare queen, and drug dealing mindsets" are readily brought to the front as to the cause of why "on average, Black men die more than seven years earlier than do US women of all races, and Black men die younger than all other groups of men, except Native Americans."[6] The blatant health disparity for Black men is all the proof we need to show that we have been "cut off from the land of the living." The federal government's silence and the multi-billion-dollar healthcare system is all the answer we need to Isaiah's question, "Who of his generation protested?" Not one. We can blame Black men for our plight until the cows come home, but the plate tectonics of the world past and present that men of color are born into is deeply rooted in recent and not recent past. Indeed, "the legacy of slavery is a root cause . . . forms of discrimination such as Jim Crow, lynching, de facto segregation, and the prison industrial complex, enacted against Black Americans in contemporary U.S. society are enduring versions of institutional forces that manufacture and maintain health disparities."[7] Compartmentalizing present realities from history will disconnect us from the ever present cause and effect variables of racism. To construct a better future and a better world, we must face history and ourselves.

Eugenics: When Science Is Converted to the Beliefs of the Scientist

So insidious is bigotry that it must make up evidence to support its claim that some are inferior and others superior. Eugenics, defined by one of its founders, Francis Galton, is "the science which deals with all influences that improve the inborn qualities of a race; also with those that develop them to the utmost advantage."[8] After several decades of baseless science and claims, this same pseudo-science was adopted by the Nazis as evidentiary support for their "pure" Aryan race. Respected scientists (Davenport) and organizations like the Carnegie Institute signed on and funded eugenics research against Blacks, the poor, individuals with disabilities, and those suffering from mental illnesses in the United States. Carnegie eventually conceded that the funding of such projects began in 1902. It wasn't until 1944 that the Carnegie Institute ended its involvement in the eugenics program. Posted on the Carnegie website is a confessional letter. It reads in part:

> Since then, we have expressed our institutional distress over the impact of these actions by attempting to distance ourselves from our involvement in this morally reprehensible endeavor. There is no excuse, then or now, for our institution's previous willingness to empower researchers who sought to pervert scientific inquiry to justify their own racist and ableist prejudices. Our support of eugenics made us complicit in driving decades of brutal and unconscionable actions by governments in the United States and around the world. As the President of the Carnegie Institution for Science, I want to express my sincere and profound apologies for this organization's past involvement in these horrific pseudoscientific activities.[9]

In the early twentieth century, educator and eugenicist Harry Laughlin championed sterilization, maintaining that some 10 percent of Americans were defective and should not be allowed to procreate. In *Buck v. Bell*, the Supreme Court ruled that sterilizing people based on the (false) science of eugenics was constitutional. Oliver Wendell Holmes, writing for the Court's opinion, said, "It is better for all the world if, instead of waiting to execute degenerate offspring for crime or to let them starve for their imbecility, society can prevent those who are manifestly unfit from continuing their kind."[10] Eugenics was also used to support laws prohibiting interracial marriage. Under these laws, biracial children were deemed illegitimate and thus had no legal claim to the inheritance of their White fathers. Eugenics was used to justify the sanctioned illiteracy of Blacks. It was used to justify labeling Blacks as subhuman. It was used to justify barring immigrants from certain countries from entering the United States. Former president Donald Trump employed eugenics-type language calling nations in Africa "shithole countries." He vociferously opposed allowing individuals from Latin America and Africa to immigrate to the United States, maintaining that we should instead welcome immigrants from places like Norway. The working assumption that society is constantly progressing towards Abraham Lincoln's better angels is just not true. Democracy is fragile, and the ghosts of oppression are always with us and must be guarded against at all times.

A Salacious Lie: Black People Are Less Susceptible to Pain

On November 29, 2020, Susan Moore, a medical doctor specializing in family and geriatric medicine, tested positive for COVID-19 and was admitted to IU Health North Hospital in Carmel, Indiana. Originally from Jamaica, Dr. Moore migrated to the United States and, like so many others, pushed past racism and other obstacles and claimed her piece of the American Dream. On December 4, 2020, from her hospital bed, she sent out a video of her experience that went viral. The treating physicians consistently downplayed the seriousness of her condition and the severity of her pain. In the video, she says that after begging for pain relievers, the doctor told her that he was not comfortable giving her more narcotics. "I was crushed," she said. "He made me feel like I was a drug addict. And, he knew I was a physician. I don't take narcotics. I was hurting." Even Remdesivir, one of the most effective drugs treating COVID-19, was given to her only sparingly. She was told that she did not need it because she did not appear to have shortness of breath. She begged them to send her to another hospital if they weren't going to give her the proper treatment. This was after being told that she could go home because her illness wasn't that severe. "This is how Black people get killed," she said. "When you send them home and they don't know how to fight for themselves . . . I put forth and I maintain if I was White, I wouldn't have to go through that [experience]." On December 20, 2020, Dr. Susan Moore died from COVID-19 related complications. In response to her deathbed accusations, IU Health North Hospital claimed that they took the allegations seriously:

> Treatment options are often agreed upon and reviewed by medical experts from a variety of specialties, and we stand by the commitment and expertise of our caregivers and the quality of care delivered to our patients every day.[11]

Dr. Moore's death belies the hospital's claims of excellence. She was ignored, denied pain medicine, and overlooked by patient advocates. Elie Wiesel said it best: "The opposite of love is not hate, it's indifference. The opposite of art is not ugliness, it's indifference. The opposite of faith is not heresy, it's indifference. And the opposite of life is not death, it's indifference."[12]

Dr. Moore mattered little to the hospital system that she gave her life to. The video sent chills down the spine of many Black folks because we know that if she, a doctor, could not convince the hospital to give her proper care, then "What chance do the rest of us have?" Her death exposes a truth that Black folks have always known. There is a great disparity in the field of healthcare. Race is always a factor. It's a matter of life and death—sometimes more death than life.

In September 2004, my 2-year-old daughter Vanessa developed a severe rash. My wife took her to the pediatrician who diagnosed her with a form of eczema and prescribed a topical cream. We used the cream as directed but the scratching continued. When she began sneezing and coughing, I decided to take her to the doctor myself. I explained my concerns and told him that her stomach felt hard upon palpation. He examined her and agreed. "This child has an enlarged liver," he said. We rushed her to the hospital and shortly thereafter discovered that she had a large malignancy in her liver. Our suspicion of the medical community goes beyond a history of not obtaining the best possible care. It goes beyond the eugenic projects of the last century. Disparity in healthcare is very much at play today.

Remember John Brown: A Man Who Lived to Tell the Tale

Susan Moore's experience was hardly an isolated incident. Such atrocities have been happening in the medical community for hundreds of years. In 1847, John Brown, a runaway enslaved man who, after decades of being tortured by his physician owner, Dr. Thomas Hamilton, told the story about the tortures he endured. Brown was a human lab rat. He was purposely exposed to severe heat repeatedly in an effort to find the cure for heat stroke. "Hamilton used Brown to try to determine how deep black skin went, believing it was thicker than White skin."[13] John Brown escaped and eventually made his way to England and freedom. He writes, "The little I have told may afford an insight into the system of Slavery, but it is only a 'small peep.' I have suffered enough myself, but others have endured and are daily enduring, perhaps, much more."[14]

The 1619 Project, a long-form journalism series comprised of "essays and other pieces that demonstrate how slavery—and the racial discrimination that followed—has shaped every aspect of modern life, from health care to public transportation,"[15] exposed the sadistic and maniacal practices of Dr. Benjamin Moseley, a British doctor practicing in the Caribbean in the 18th century. In 1792, he published *A Treatise on Tropical Diseases: On Military Operations; and on the Climate.* In it, he wrote, "What would be the cause of insupportable pain to a White man, a Negro would almost disregard." He continued, "I have amputated the legs of many Negroes who have held the upper part of the limb themselves."[16]

Moseley's work illustrates one of most reprehensible byproducts of racism. It obliterates empathy. In the mind of the racist, humanity belongs only to him and "his kind." Thus, he is not compelled to treat the victim of his prejudice with any compassion or decency. He does not empathize with the oppressed because the oppressed has no claim on humanity. The racist does not need to justify his medical experiments on the "less-sentient." It is not that difficult to draw a line connecting the sadistic experiments of Benjamin Moseley and Thomas Hamilton to the racism infecting the medical community today. Susan Moore's senseless death and my daughter's gross misdiagnosis bear witness to this. The threads of history are always with us. The problem is that far too often we do not make the connections. I firmly believe that in order to express appropriate outrage and lobby for change, we must be able to make and show historical connections. Dr. Moore's deathbed plea for more medicine is connected directly to doctors who are the recipients of what Benjamin Moseley and Thomas Hamilton taught— Black people feel less pain.

Addressing the Disparities in Treating Black Pain

Despite advances in medical technology, assessing physical pain has remained a subjective and self-reported endeavor. In a way, doctors have to believe (or not) what patients tell them about their levels of pain. If the treating physician has certain preconceived ideas or misconceptions about a patient, that is, Blacks are more likely to abuse pain medicine, then that bias is going to impact that patient's believability and thus whether or not pain medication is prescribed. Raymond C. Tait and John T. Chibnall of Saint Louis University School of Medicine in their article, *Racial/Ethnic Disparities in the Assessment and Treatment of Pain,* point out several variables or contributing factors at work that decide patient outcome. I would like to examine four of these variables (see Figure 3.1).

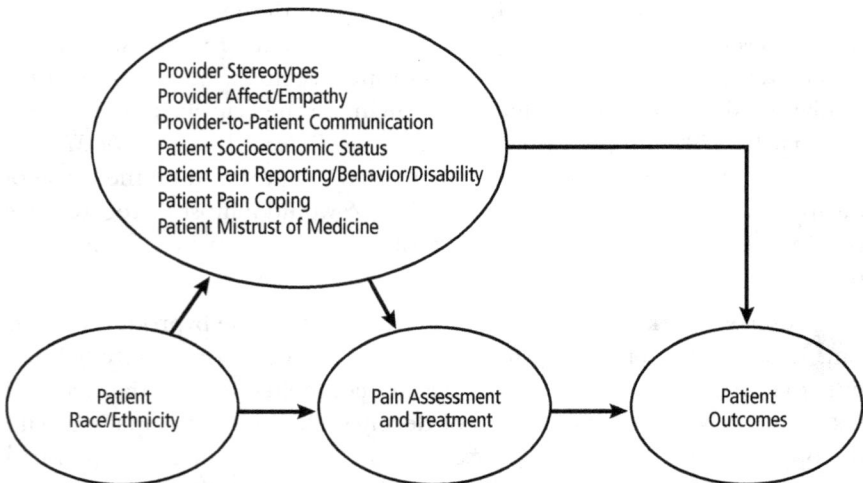

Provider Stereotypes
Provider Affect/Empathy
Provider-to-Patient Communication
Patient Socioeconomic Status
Patient Pain Reporting/Behavior/Disability
Patient Pain Coping
Patient Mistrust of Medicine

Patient
Race/Ethnicity

Pain Assessment
and Treatment

Patient
Outcomes

Figure 3.1 Factors contribting to racial/ethnic disparities in pain assessment, treatment, and outcome.

- *The Provider Stereotypes.* The authors note that while physicians denied racial bias when treating Black patients—specifically for their pain management—the research proves otherwise.[17] There is nothing new or surprising here. Racists often try to "prove" that they are not racist. "I have friends that are Black," is an oft used counter measure of the "racially enlightened" White person. The equivocation would be laughable if it wasn't so sad. As if the remedy to racism is having a few Black friends. A person denying that he or she is not racist does not make this true. The authors make this point clear. When surveyed, medical students said all the right things, but when observed in the field, their behaviors said differently. Teachers that think Black and Brown children are incapable of achieving priority learning standards will never teach them those standards. Doctors who ask patients of color to describe their pain on a scale of 1 to 10 will never hear 10/10 if their hearts are hardened to their suffering.

- *The Provider Affect or Empathy.* Consider Dr. Bonnic, the treating physician of Dr. Susan Moore. It didn't matter to Bonnic what Moore said. It didn't matter that she was an expert in the field. It didn't matter that she had years of training and experience. Bonnic believed what he believed about her before she walked into that hospital. In his mind, she did not need pain medication, was undeserving of Remdesivir. Susan Moore was not the first Black patient that Bonnic denied proper treatment to, nor will she be the last. Racism poisons the mind of its host. Recently, I went to a local pharmacy in Getty Square, Yonkers to get my COVID-19 booster shot. The pharmacy occupied a tiny space that simply did not have the room to administer the booster with any amount of patient confidentiality let alone privacy. Seemingly oblivious to HIPAA or, really, basic social etiquette, the pharmacist bid me roll up my sleeve with some four other people standing literally inches away. Appalled that I would point out this blatant violation, he tersely suggested I was free to wait until the line got shorter if I had an issue with privacy. I told him that my objection was not a matter of personal preference, it was about basic human dignity, about the rights of all the people that were in that space. In the end, I left the pharmacy not having received the shot. The following day I took my 6-year-old daughter to the public library for her COVID-19 shot where there were partitions and privacy.

- *Provider–Patient Communication.* If pain is subjective, then the communication between patient and physician must be built on trust. The physician must trust that the patient is giving an honest account of his pain, that an 8/10 is truly an 8/10 *for that particular patient.* Likewise, the patient must trust that the physician is acting in his best interests, like, for example, when an alternative pain management therapy is suggested. Obstacles like language barriers and cultural differences can negatively affect patient/ doctor communication. An additional barrier might also be the abysmally low number of Black men entering medical school.

> Research data continue to reveal increasingly high rates of adverse life experiences with respect to Black males. While Black males matriculate to medical school at a low rate, they experience racial discrimination and pervasive health disparities with morbidity and mortality at a high rate. We believe the current state of society represents not just a crisis among Black men, but in fact an American crisis.[18]

A drum that I will beat again and again is this: All people need visions and images of themselves represented in the places that they frequent. This is why, after my daughter's pediatrician mishandled her symptoms and diagnosis, it was important to both Senikha and me that we find a doctor we could communicate with and who understood our culture. To date, we have recommended many of our friends and family members to our Caribbean-born pediatrician and his daughter. Each time I enter the practice, I feel a sense of ease and community. I have had no such luck finding primary care physicians in my community that are African American males.

■ *Patient Socioeconomic Status.* In the United States, socioeconomics is often linked to the quality of healthcare we receive. Variables such as geographical locations are tied to income opportunities, access to quality healthcare facilities, and the wait time to see a physician. Additionally, having private vs. public insurance often affects which exams doctors are willing to perform. This, of course, not only weakens the trust between doctor and patient, it also puts the patient's health at risk. More, if men know that their insurance coverage is limited, they are less likely to go to the doctor lest they receive a bill that they are unable to pay. Many men wait until their pain becomes so unbearable they have no choice but to go to the emergency room. By that time, their illness has often progressed to the point that life-saving intervention is necessary. This further burdens the healthcare system and significantly increases the mortality rate of Black men. Madeline

Ohlson, in her article, "Effects of Socioeconomic Status and Race on Access to Healthcare in the United States," notes,

> As low SES minority groups suffer from a lack of adequate healthcare, they also face the mentioned stigma associated with a lack of insurance. Due to this stigma, prescription drug use is lower for Black communities partly because the physicians resort to prescribing differential drugs, due to a sense of mistrust and prejudice, which is ultimately harmful to the patient's health as some medications could be necessary as treatment."[19]

Conclusion

Sankofa is a powerful concept in the Akan Twi and Fante languages in Ghana. It means, *it is not a taboo to go back and fetch that which is at risk of being left behind.* Black men have been left behind since the first enslaved Africans arrived on the shores of the Virginia coast. There is little hope that even after 400 years in this land, we will ever have true equality. We as a people must courageously retrieve all that has been taken—including our heritage and dignity. In order to do this, we need to be healthy. And, the research is clear about the state of Black men's health in America. "Of all racial/ethnic groups in the US, Black men continue to have the shortest life expectancy. Furthermore, when it comes to the leading causes of death and disability within US society, Black men suffer disproportionately."[20]

It is an indisputable fact that, of all ethnic and racial groups in the United States, Black men have the shortest lifespan. And, while it is easy to blame risk behaviors—substance use and abuse, smoking, community violence, unsafe driving, to name a few—we should never ignore the impact of racism and discrimination on the life expectancy of Black men. When considering such factors as the suspension rate of young Black men, high school dropout rate, incarceration rate, unemployment rate, and other data points, we tend to look at the individual or at Black men as a group rather than structural and institutional racism. The research shows that the primary illnesses that sweep Black men from this earth include (a) heart disease, (b) hypertension, (c) prostate cancer, (d) diabetes, and (e) HIV/AIDS. We must reach out and reclaim our health even in the midst of the unprecedented and sustained assault on the Black body for over 400 years. We have survived this long, not by chance, but by an indelible will to live. We must work together as a people to combat the legacy of eugenics that, even today, continues to subversively influence provider care. We must do our best to empower each other first and do our best to be good stewards of the only body we will ever have. Community organizations, faith communities, and public institutions must make men's health a priority. Sermons should encourage holistic care of body, mind, spirit, and family. We must probe the quality of care given to those in our communities and challenge care providers to optimize their care to our people. Dr. Susan Moore's death should not be in vain. Let her dying message be a clarion call to all of us. We should not die because of the color of our skin. We should not die early because of the zip code that we live in. We should not be given diminished care because of the type of health insurance we do or do not have. If *Sankofa* is reaching back and fetching the things that are at risk of being left behind, then our health should be at the top of the list. We need interventions at the micro, mezzo, and especially macro levels.

Notes

1. James H. Jones, "The Tuskegee Legacy AIDS and the Black Community," *The Hastings Center Report* 22, no. 6 (1992): 38–40.
2. Allan M. Brandt, "Racism and Research: The Case of the Tuskegee Syphilis Study," *Hastings Center Report* (1978): 21–29.
3. Hippocratic Oath.
4. Jason Wasserman, M. A. Flannery, and J. M. Clair. "Raising the Ivory Tower: The Production of Knowledge and Distrust of Medicine among African Americans," *Journal of Medical Ethics* 33, no. 3 (2007): 177–180.
5. James H. Jones, "The Tuskegee Legacy AIDS and the Black Community," *The Hastings Center Report* 22, no. 6 (1992): 38–40.
6. Keon L. Gilbert, Rashawn Ray, Arjumand Siddiqi, Shivan Shetty, Elizabeth A. Baker, Keith Elder, and Derek M. Griffith, "Visible and Invisible Trends in Black Men's Health: Pitfalls and Promises for Addressing Racial, Ethnic, and Gender Inequities in Health," *Annual Review of Public Health* 37 (2016): 295–311.
7. Ibid.
8. Francis Galton, "Eugenics: Its Definition, Scope, and Aims," *American Journal of Sociology* 10, no. 1 (1904): 1–25.
9. Eric Isaacs, "Carnegie Institution for Science Statement on Eugenics Research," Carnegie Institution for Science, accessed August 28, 2022 from: https://carnegiescience.edu/carnegie-institution-science-statement-eugenics-research.
10. J. Jackson, Nadine M. Weidman, and Gretchen Rubin. "The Origins of Scientific Racism," *The Journal of Blacks in Higher Education* 50 (2005): 66–79.
11. Doctor dies of COVID-19 after filming viral video: "This is how Black people get killed" | The Hill
12. Elie Wiesel, Eric Liu, and Nick Hanauer, "Arts Education as/for Artistic Citizenship," *Artistic Citizenship: Artistry, Social Responsibility, and Ethical Praxis* (2016): 81.

13. Linda Villarosa, "Myths about How Physical Racial Differences Were Used to Justify Slavery—And Are Still Believed by Doctors Today," *The New York Times* August 14, 2019, www.nytimes.com/interactive/2019/08/14/magazine/racial -differencesdoctors.html.

14. Louis Alexis Chamerovzow, "Slave Life in Georgia: A Narrative of the Life, Sufferings and Escape of John Brown, a Fugitive Slave Now in England," London: [British and Foreign Anti-Slavery Society] (1855).

15. WNYC News, "In '1619' Project, the Times Puts Slavery Front and Center of the American Experience," August 16, 2019, https://www.wnyc.org/story/ new-york-times-1619-project/.

16. Benjamin Moseley, *A Treatise on Tropical Diseases: On Military Operations; and on the Climate* (1792).

17. Irene Blair, Edward Havranek, David Price, Rebecca Hanratty, Diane Fairclough, Tillman Farley, Holen Hirsh, and John Steiner, "Assessment of Biases against Latinos and African Americans among Primary Care Providers and Community Members," *American Journal of Public Health* 103, no. 1 (2013): 92–98; Anthony Greenwald, Brian A. Nosek, and Mahzarin R. Banaji. "Understanding and using the implicit association test: I. An Improved Scoring Algorithm," *Journal of Personality and Social Psychology* 85, no. 2 (2003): 197.

18. Cato T. Laurencin and Marsha Murray, "An American Crisis: The Lack of Black Men in Medicine," *Journal of Racial and Ethnic Health Disparities* 4, no. 3 (2017): 317–321.

19. Madeline Ohlson, "Effects of Socioeconomic Status and Race on Access to Healthcare in the United States," *Perspectives* 12, no. 1 (2020): 2.

20. Letisha Engracia Cardoso Brown, "Eat to Live, Don't Live to Eat: Black Men, Masculinity, Faith and Food," *International Journal of Environmental Research and Public Health* 17, no. 12 (2020): 4264.

$$4$$

Black Men's Mental Health

Men, and Black men in particular, have waged a long battle with mental health on many fronts. From the misguided notion that we must hide our emotions and emotional pain to inaccessible mental health support, Black men across all socioeconomic demographics are often the last to seek or receive quality mental health intervention. The research is detailed: "Men in the United States are four times more likely than women to commit suicide, yet have lower prevalence rates for major depression and other depressive disorders."[1] This startling data point tells us that men, while less likely to experience or, better yet, to express mental health struggles, are far more likely to complete suicide. This is partly because of what Benita Chatmon, assistant dean for clinical nursing education at LSU Health-New Orleans School of Nursing, and others call "the other silent killer." She notes, "Mental health among men often goes untreated because they are far less likely to seek mental health treatment than women. Depression and suicide are ranked as a leading cause of death among men." Not only that, "Six million men are affected by depression in the United States every year. Men (79 percent of 38,364) die by suicide at a rate four times higher than

No Country For Black Men, pages 45–68
Copyright © 2023 by Information Age Publishing
www.infoagepub.com

TABLE 4.1 Likely Suicide Methods Among Men and Women	
Suicide Method in Men	Suicide Method in Women
1. Firearms 2. Hanging 3. Asphyxiation or suffocation 4. Jumping 5. Moving objects 6. Sharp objects 7. Vehicle exhaust gas	1. Self-poisoning 2. Exsanguination (bleeding out from a cut such as a "slit wrist") 3. Drowning 4. Hanging 5. Firearms

women."[2] The data is consistent. While women are more likely than men to report mental health struggles and more likely to attempt suicide, men are more likely to *complete* suicide. "Despite increased outreach over the last decade, depressed African American men are significantly less likely to seek help compared with depressed White men."[3] Table 4.1 shows such likely suicide methods among men and women.[4]

We carry our traumas with us. They lodge themselves in our psyche, in our bodies. We live out such traumas in developing survival mechanisms that in some instances save our lives and in others hasten our death.

Confronting the Myths About Suicide

Suicide is preventable. Myths such as "talking about suicide will plant suicidal ideas" perpetuate the vacuum of ignorance about suicide prevention. Many people still believe that anyone who expresses suicidal ideation is bent on dying. This is simply not true. Suicidal persons often just want the pain to go away. Address the source of their pain, provide early intervention, and the risk of suicide significantly decreases. One of the most common myths about people who express suicidal ideation is that they do so simply to gain attention. This myth is dangerous. It discounts the catalyst for suicidal thoughts and behaviors. Thus, intervention is not provided, and the risk of suicide increases. Helpguide.org lists some of the myths and facts about suicide. Here are just a few:

Myth: People Who Talk About Suicide Won't Really Do It

Fact: Almost everyone who attempts suicide has given some clue or warning. Don't ignore even indirect references to death or suicide. Statements like, "You'll be sorry when I'm gone," "I can't see any way out"—no matter if said casually or jokingly—may indicate serious suicidal feelings.

Myth: If Someone Is Intent on Suicide, Nothing Is Going to Stop Them

Fact: Even a severely depressed person has mixed feelings about death, fluctuating between wanting to live and wanting to die. Rather than wanting death, they just want the pain to stop.

Myth: People Who Die by Suicide Are People Who Were Unwilling to Seek Help

Fact: Many people try to get help before attempting suicide. In fact, studies show that more than 50 percent of suicide victims sought medical help in the 6 months prior to their deaths.

Myth: Talking About Suicide May Give Someone the Idea

Fact: You don't give someone suicidal ideas by talking about suicide. Rather, the opposite is true. Talking openly and honestly about suicidal thoughts and feelings can help save a life.

Many years ago, I visited a friend in the psychiatric unit at a hospital. While sitting in the common area speaking with my friend, I overheard a conversation between an elderly woman and her adult son. This African American man, who appeared to be in his early thirties, was obviously in tremendous psychological and emotional pain. He was angry. He was not well. He accused his mother of knowing about the abuse he suffered at the hands of his father and did nothing to stop it. She sat across the table from him and wept. No amount of tears moved him to reconsider his perspective. She reached across to hold his hand, but he pulled away physically, emotionally, and spiritually. She simply could not reach him. She tried to tell him that she was not aware of the abuse. He was not having it. She expressed sorrow and pleaded for his forgiveness, but he could not or would not hear her. He told her that there were many buildings in Coop City in the Bronx and that one way or another he was going to jump off one of them. He told her that he did not want to live any longer. Like so many families, this one was torn apart by abuse and mental illness. It has been almost twenty years since I sat in that hospital room and became an unwitting interloper in another's tragic story. In a way, I was there to bear witness to the incalculable suffering of a mother and a son. I still think about that young man. I think about the helplessness that bled from the mother's pleas, the guilt that she must have felt listening to his accusation, "You saw what he was doing to me, and you never defended me. You never spoke up for me."

This is a difficult chapter to write. The subject of mental health is complex and hard to talk about. But I am reminded, "That which we cannot put into words we cannot put to rest." We must find the courage to put into words things that are deemed shameful, painful, taboo. Too often, families hide the cause of death when the cause of death is suicide. In this chapter, my goal is to review the literature and data on mental health among men, and Black men in particular, with the goal of naming the challenges and opportunities to support my brothers.

The Adverse Childhood Experiences from 3,000 Feet

The Adverse Childhood Experiences (ACE) was a large study conducted from 1995 to 1997. Some (mostly White) 9,508 participants were given a comprehensive physical examination followed by a survey about any negative childhood experiences they endured in their family life. The researchers focused on eight types of trauma:

1. Psychological abuse
2. Physical abuse
3. Sexual abuse
4. Violence against the mother
5. Substance abuse at home
6. Mental illness
7. Suicide attempts by family members
8. History of incarceration by family members

The results of this confidential survey were then juxtaposed against the results of the comprehensive health examination that assessed behavior, health status, and disease outcomes. As you might imagine, the results were revelatory for both medical and behavioral health practitioners across the country and indeed around the world. The research revealed a direct correlation between ACEs and physical health, risky behaviors, substance use and abuse, and even early death. For example, "Persons who had experienced four or more categories of childhood exposure, compared to those who had experienced none, had 4- to 12-fold increase health risks for alcoholism, drug abuse, depression, and suicide attempt."[5] Those impacted by the more negative categories such as sexual and physical abuse were likely to be heavy smokers, in poor health, and had greater than fifty sexual partners at the time of the study. They were also more likely to be living with some form of STI, obesity, heart disease, cancer, or lung and liver diseases.

Often, when we discuss how childhood experiences impact our longevity and quality of life, we anchor the conversation around parenting and familial traumas. For Black men, another factor plays a central role. Systemic racism, in all sectors of society, continues to shape the lived experiences and health outcomes of men of color.

This groundbreaking research shows that childhood experiences, particularly traumatic ones, stay with us if not properly dealt with. This type of trauma continues to grow, like a wart that feeds from our flesh and blood. The problem with the ACE study is that it only cursorily examined the impact of institutional racism on people of color. It, like so many other studies, mutes the institutional trauma that Black and Brown people living in the United States face from the moment they are born.

The ACE study should have changed the landscape of public health policies. And, to a large degree it has. Unfortunately, this study had very few Black and Brown participants. Of the 13,494 surveys sent out and the 9,508 respondents, 5 percent were African American, and some 75 percent were White. There are significant implications in omitting our lived experiences in such a body of work. More, the study focused primarily on the impact of specific issues on the family (issues such as physical, sexual, and substance abuse) and on the individual while neglecting institutional variables and their impacts on both the family and the individual. For example, one survey question asked if a family member had ever been incarcerated. The answer to that question will more likely be yes for African Americans than for White Americans. Why is this so? Because in this country, people with mental health conditions make up 64 percent of the jailed population.

> Black people with mental health conditions, particularly schizophrenia, bipolar disorder, and other psychoses are more likely to be incarcerated than people of other races. Black people make up a mere 9.6 percent of the population in Los Angeles, yet they constitute 31 percent of LA County Jail inmates, and 43.7 percent of those diagnosed with serious mental illness requiring special jail housing.[6]

Why? Because negative stereotypes are woven into the fabric of American culture, evidenced in part by the racial profiling of Black men as well as by the social behaviors displayed by White Americans when they encounter Black men in public places (e.g., purse clutching). Most conversations with White Americans about the incarceration rate of Black men quickly veer in the direction of the nature and character of African American men rather than what is long known by scholars and ordinary folks alike. "Some scholars have linked the percentage of African American men in prisons not only to the perception of them as criminals but also to aggressive policing tactics, as well as to the overwhelming presence of law enforcement in pre-dominantly African American neighborhoods,"[7] says Greer and Cavalhieri. The authors point out that more Black men are disproportionately targeted and victimized by police.

The ACE study brings an oft overlooked truth into focus. Human suf-fering doesn't take place in a vacuum. Like child abuse and neglect, racism not only informs but forms our lived experiences. Bessel Van Der Kolk, in his bestselling book, *The Body Keeps the Score: Brain, Mind, and Body in the Healing of Trauma,* compares soldiers engaged in warfare for a limited time and children exposed to persistent trauma at home and the impact of such traumas on the mind, body, and soul. Van Der Kolk brilliantly argues that if a man can develop PTSD, depression, suicide, and the like, after mere months at war, "How much greater is the psychological impact of years of abuse on a child?"[8] To this I would add, "What about Black men who have been exposed to persistent violence at the hands of society simply for being Black?" We are reminded that such violence is perpetrated against Black males the moment they enter the world. We have all the evidence that we need to assess this claim. It is housed in public school classrooms, in penitentiaries, in our absence from college lecture halls. The evidence is present in the relentless obstacles that bar us from enjoying our share of the American dream.

Greer and Cavalhieri argue[9] that the impact of racism on Black men has not been examined adequately. The research that does exist is segmented. Some have attempted to look at how healthcare systems treat and deal with Black men. Others have been interested in Black men's encounters with law enforcement. Still others have focused on obstacles young Black men face in colleges or the overrepresentation of young men of color being given special education designation or the disproportionate suspension rates of Black boys. What has not been done is a comprehensive analysis of how all these systems working in concert have diminished the outcomes for Black men. Additionally, and to the overarching purpose of this chapter, what has not been looked at adequately is the impact of racism on the mental health of Black men in the United States.

Mental Illness Diagnosis and the Dreaded 911 Call

Remember this name: Daniel T. Prude. Black. Male. Diagnosed with mental illness. Killed by police. Remember. A study done by The Treatment Ad-vocacy Center revealed, "The risk of being killed while being approached or stopped by law enforcement in the community is 16 times higher for individuals with untreated serious mental illness than for other civilians." The research further reveals, "By most conservative estimates, at least 1 in 4 fatal law enforcement encounters involve an individual with serious mental illness."[10] Already a target for harassment, racial profiling, and police brutality, Black men are more likely than any other demographic to be involved (read: be killed) in such encounters. Add in the variable of a mental illness and that "likelihood" becomes more of a foregone conclusion. Black men are already seen as dangerous, less than, violent, and a menace to society. They are already less likely to seek mental health care and, when they do, the care they receive is inadequate. Research shows, "Non-Hispanic Black and Hispanic men (26.4 percent) were about 40 percent less likely than non-Hispanic White men (45.4 percent) to have used mental health treatments."[11] Daniel T. Prude never stood a chance. You see, Daniel was visiting his brother, Joe, in Rochester, New York when he experienced a psychotic episode. With a history of psychosis and addiction, Daniel was constantly in and out of treatment. In the days leading up to his encounter with the police, he had been hospitalized for stepping into the path of a moving train and diving head-first down a staircase. Daniel was taken to the hospital and released without being admitted. His brother could not understand how Strong Memorial Hospital could release an obviously disturbed, suicidal man. Four hours later, Daniel disappeared. Joe called 911 at 3:00 am on March 30th, 2020 asking for help finding his brother. By 3:20 a.m., the police found Daniel walking in the street completely naked and talking to himself. It was 30 degrees.

That early morning encounter with the police would be Daniel's last. On March 30th, Daniel Prude, like so many other men of color, died in police custody. The firestorm that followed brought into focus not only how the entire public service system failed Daniel, but what we know all too well: There's no country for Black men in America.

One officer's body cam was the only witness to the injustice perpetrated by police on the streets of Rochester that early spring morning. After being cuffed and made to sit in the middle of the road, police placed a "spit hood" over Daniel's head because he was spitting on them. This further agitated Prude who was in the middle of a psychotic episode. At one point, as he struggled to get the hood off, several officers could be seen laughing at and mocking him, as though his life had no meaning, as though his dark skin was impervious to the below freezing temperature or the asphalt that he was sitting on, naked. These images tell the brutal truth about who the savage is in this scenario, and it's not Daniel. I know I'm not the only one to see this sick hypocrisy that's been allowed to infect our country for centuries. Our country that champions freedom. Our country that isn't truly ours because it's no country for Black men.

Head pressed against the pavement for two minutes, knees in his back, head covered by a bag, hands tightly cuffed behind him, Daniel had no chance of showing those officers that he, too, was a human being. He had no way of appealing to their humanity because they did not see him as human. He had no way of appealing to God because, in that instance, God abandoned him like He has abandoned so many Black men during their encounters with police.

Daniel Prude's naked body lay motionless as EMTs worked in vain to resuscitate him. They searched for a pulse, felt his skin, and said he was "pretty cold." CPR commenced as the ambulance returned to the same institution that had just discharged him. The coroner's report stated that he died of asphyxia. What it should have said is that he died of racism.

Daniel's case is but one among countless Black men suffering from mental illness who've fallen victim to systemic racism. Eudes Pierre, age twenty-six, of Crown Heights, Brooklyn was known to have a mental illness. On December 20, 2021, he charged at police with a knife and was shot and killed. A suicide note was later discovered.

Shaheed Vassell, an immigrant from Jamaica, was a welder who struggled with mental illness. A 911 call was made on April 4, 2018 about a man waving a metal object. Shaheed was gunned down. A piece of a metal pipe was found where his blood seeped from his veins.

Stephon Clark encountered police after a report of vandalism was called in. When officers tried to approach him, he ran. One of those officers yelled, "Gun, gun, gun!" When the smoke settled, Stephon was found dead in his grandmother's backyard. A cell phone, *not* a gun, was recovered at the scene.

As tragic and unnecessary as these cases are, what happened to Daniel was worse. The officers couldn't claim they were in danger. They didn't fear for their lives. There would be no conjured-up stories that they had to use deadly force because Daniel reached for their weapons. How could he? He was naked, cuffed, blindfolded, and cold.

Daniel's death is not a testament to his "depraved" life. He wasn't a criminal. Neither is his death a testament to his questionable choices or his poor decision making. He suffered from mental illness. Blaming Daniel's death on his mental illness would be as unconscionable as blaming a rape victim for dressing provocatively. Daniel didn't die because his brother called 911—though I am sure that he will be living with the unnecessary guilt of having placed that call. He died because the hospital released a man who manifested suicidal ideation. He died because those who swore to protect and serve failed to see his humanity, so they killed him. At the press conference that followed, the mayor of Rochester conceded that had Daniel been a White man, he would not have been killed.

A Call for Parity Now: Mental Illness and the Desperate Need for Treatment

According to the National Alliance on Mental Illness (NAMI):

> Mental health parity describes the equal treatment of mental health conditions and substance use disorders in insurance plans. When a plan has parity, it means that if you are provided unlimited doctor visits for a chronic condition like diabetes, then they must offer unlimited visits for a mental health condition such as depression or schizophrenia.[12]

It is no secret that mental illnesses are not treated the same as physical ones. Let's say you fall and break your hand. You would report to the local emergency room where a doctor would do assessments, x-rays, cast the broken bone, monitor progress, and, at some point, remove the cast. Physical therapy might even follow. It's unlikely you would do the same thing for a mental disorder. Consider the following scenario: You're chatting with a few colleagues at an informal work gathering. The inevitable topic of aches and pains comes up as it tends to do at such functions—let's face it, none of us is getting any younger. A member of the group, we'll call him Eric, mentions he has to make an appointment with a cardiologist as he was just diagnosed with atrial fibrillation. Another, let's call him Phillip, pipes up and says he needs to see his psychiatrist because the medication he takes for bipolar disorder makes him feel drowsy all the time. Without overthinking it, "What, if any, judgments do you make about the two individuals? Does one admission make you more uncomfortable than the other? What do you think about the value of the MD behind the psychiatrist's name versus the MD behind the cardiologist's?" A few days later, you accompany Eric to the pharmacy to pick up a new prescription, Diltiazem, for his afib. While you're there, you bump into Phillip who's getting his antipsychotic medication, Haloperidol. Ultimately, Eric's afib stabilizes and Phillip succumbs to his BPD, jumping from the roof of his apartment building to his death. Is Eric lucky? Was Phillip simply weak?

Later in this chapter, we will get to issues of insurance and access to treatment as well as responsive treatment and mental health parity. But first, we must confront the taboos surrounding mental health and its root causes. Even today, there are those who believe that mental illnesses are rooted in demonic possession. Dmitri N. Shalin notes, "This manifestation of demonic power was based on the belief that demons could enter the bodies of human beings against their will and take control of their physical movements and mental facilities."[13] Such beliefs continue to impact how we view mental illness, and, even more, how we respond to those who are afflicted by it. Many people have not reconciled the distance between mental illness as a spiritual matter and a physio-psychological disorder. For some, this binary stance has further alienated those struggling with mental health from much needed treatment and the quality life that they so deserve.

When I was a young man in my mid-twenties, I was invited to speak at a small storefront church in the Bronx. Close to the end of my sermon, a middle-aged woman wandered in from the street. She appeared to be in the middle of a psychotic episode. She was disheveled, her hair was matted, and she was mumbling something incoherent. She was immediately brought to the front of the service to be prayed over. That was the best gift the leadership of the congregation felt that they could offer this woman. We prayed for her feverishly. Some prayed for healing, others passionately commanded demons to take flight. The prayer seemed like it would never end. Those praying expected a particular result, and when it didn't happen, they prayed harder. When it still didn't happen, someone reached for a bottle of olive oil commonly used for anointing the forehead. They attempted to pour the oil down the woman's throat as their way of performing an exorcism. I grabbed the minister's hand as he violently thrust the bottle into the woman's mouth. I told him he couldn't do this. He looked at me as though I was out of order, as though I was preventing this stranger—someone's mother, sister, daughter—from being healed. I told him that he could hurt the woman. He backed down and continued the passionate prayer. Eventually, everyone ran out of steam, and the woman turned towards the same door that she came through and disappeared into the night. While it would be inappropriate to compare the murder of Daniel Prude by police officers to how this small church attempted to rid this woman of her "demons," one thing is for sure—neither church nor state responded correctly.

Effective treatment of mental illness will require a community approach that starts with educating stakeholders, de-stigmatizing mental health including the use of psychotropic medication. It will also include access to quality care not based on zip code, socioeconomic status, gender, or skin color. Additionally, we will have to concede that racism in the United States continues to have deleterious effects on men of color. Shawn O. Utsey, in his article, "Racism and the Psychological Well-being of African American Men," discusses how psychologists and other social scientists have

examined how racism impedes African Americans' ability to fully participate in the social, economic, political, and educational markets. He notes,
"More recently, however, the psychological and somatic consequences of
racism and discrimination, as experienced by African Americans on a daily
basis, has received the attention of researchers." Employing what I call lin-
guistic courage, Utsey notes:

> Racial discrimination in American society is insidious, pervasive, ubiquitous
> and, for many African Americans, the consequences of experiencing it on
> a daily basis can be deadly. Indeed, the chronic strain associated with the
> experience of racism has been implicated in the development of several po-
> tentially fatal, stress-related diseases (e.g., high blood pressure, stroke, and
> cardiovascular disease).[14]

Talk about the impact of racism on African Americans almost never
includes the psychological effects of living in spaces where you might not
be wanted or are treated less than your White counterparts.

The Psychological Impact of Being the Most Watched Group in America

One stressor for Black men brought on by racism is the incessant surveillance. Black men are the most-watched group in America today. We are
monitored in the supermarket, department store, on the highways and
walkways across this country. Cameras are trained on us; eyes monitor our
every move often out of unfounded and unjust fears. There are internal
and external costs to this constant monitoring. It is stressful to know that
you are not trusted to walk in and out of a place of business without being
viewed as a threat. More than twenty years ago, Brian Ragsdale raised some
serious questions about the psychological impact of perpetual surveillance
on Black men. In his article, "Surveillance of African American Men and
Its Possible Effect on Social, Emotional, and Psychological Functioning,"
Ragsdale notes:

> Black men are watched while driving on our nation's highways, walking on
> public streets, shopping retail stores, and while performing job duties." He
> asks, "what are social, emotional, and psychological consequences of being
> watched, to grow up and function in a society that distrusts your physicality
> (e.g., skin color, hair texture, and size of nostrils) and that might feel so
> threatened that it believes surveillance is warranted?[15]

We tend to accept things as they are, never expecting them to get better.
It's part of our collective numbness. We accept that there will be cameras

in our schools monitoring our children's every move. We tolerate cameras in the workplace as, we're told, they yield greater productivity and security. However, when was the last time you read anything about the impact of the relentless presence of cameras in our lives? One study of surveillance in the workplace revealed, "The adverse risks associated with monitoring as a reason to limit surveillance [in the] workplace [is that it] causes physical and emotional health problems in employees." The study found "a higher incidence of headaches and other physical ailments, such as backaches, wrists pain . . . moreover, monitored workers suffered greater fatigue. Psychological problems included a 12 percent increase in depression and a 15 percent increase in anxiety."[16] It's important to note that this data is from the early 1990s. Today, cameras are much more ubiquitous. We have come to accept them as part of the landscape. Black men know intuitively that we are almost always being watched. We know this when the state trooper pulls up behind us, and our anxiety (and fear) spike. We know this when we walk through the front doors of Macy's—anxiety. We know this when we walk into the office of our children's school—anxiety. And we know this when we walk into the therapist's office—anxiety. Not only are we anxious but our very presence often inspires anxiety and increased surveillance. On the other hand, the advent of cell phone cameras has changed the narrative as ordinary citizens record crimes in progress. It was the camera phone of Darnella Frazier, a teen who recorded the murder of George Floyd.

The irony is that ordinary citizens armed with high tech cameras on their cell phones are turning the spotlight on those who often unjustly monitor and target Black and Brown men. In 2014, Eric Garner's death was captured by a citizen that then gave rise to the "Black Lives Matter" Movement.

The Counselor's Barriers to Reaching African American Men in Therapy

I have lost count of the number of individuals (men and women) and couples I've met throughout my career who were disappointed and disillusioned with their counseling experiences. Some described a cultural divide that was too great and did not return after the first session. Others tell about clinicians who were either unwilling or unable to connect with them in any meaningful way and appeared too timid to challenge them to set meaningful goals. Others stated that it was simply a waste of time and money.

Counselors (psychologists, social workers, and other mental health professionals) are not immune or exempt from stereotyping or the discriminatory worldview that many Americans have about Black men. All counselors must check their biases at the door in order to be effective; this includes counselors of color. The assumption that a counselor of color is best suited for a client of color is not valid. In fact, it can be downright dangerous because the assumption short circuits the work that such counselors need to do to create a healthy therapeutic alliance or relationship with the client. I will have more to say on this later. The research is already detailed that men are less likely to voluntarily seek mental health support from a counseling professional. Karen Barone points out that this is in part due to:[17]

- *Gender Role Stereotypes.* "Connections have been made between the adherence to masculine gender socialization norms and the lack of seeking help services particularly pertaining to American ideals such as being brave, self-reliant, stoic, unemotional, not showing weakness or not appearing feminine." Barone goes on to say, "The idea here is that these conformities conflict with seeking help from professionals thus creating barriers."
- *Maladaptive Coping Strategies.* Men are more likely to turn to unhealthy coping mechanisms than their female counterparts in dealing with their depression and other mental health struggles. Such coping strategies might include substance use and abuse, burying oneself in work, or working out (which is not bad in and of itself).
- *Lack of Literacy.* If depression and its symptoms have never been explained to us then it is difficult for us to name our depressive symptoms as such. The same thing is true for anxiety and other mental health issues. It is believed that with education about mental illness, their signs and symptoms, men would be more apt to seek help. In other words, a key solution to men seeking mental health support is the educational work that needs to be done. I maintain that community organization including clinics, hospital, government entities, and faith communities can and should invest more time and resources in such educational processes.
- *Stigma.* Stigma goes with gender role stereotypes to the extent that they both are rooted in social norms and perception. We all want to fit in. We all want to feel "normal." If the social norm is that you need to seek therapy, then that norm becomes a significant deterrent to seeking and receiving help. Recently, I was interviewed by a friend who has also done youth ministries over the years and is now a senior pastor on the east coast. He spoke candidly about enrolling into therapy after becoming a pastor. He noted that the daily cares of shepherding others can take a

toll on the leader. One way to reduce this stigma is for Black leaders within our communities to shed light on our own need for mental health intervention and where we find it. This would go a long way in destigmatizing mental health support.

▪ *Lack of confidence.* Barone suggests that another deterrent to seeking mental health support is because the mental health profession (especially social work) is dominated by women (80 percent). A "female-centric" approach to treatment can serve as yet another deterrent to men seeking help.

▪ *Mistrust.* Lastly, Barone notes, men often experience the helping profession as "punitive and corrective rather than preventative." Being mandated by the courts to receive counseling services is one thing, volunteering to go to a space that lacks warmth, trust and solidarity is another matter altogether. This is in part why so many men have vacated churches, schools, and other community spaces; they don't always feel welcome.

Additionally, heterosexual men who seek counseling do so at the behest of their female partners or because it's been mandated by the court. One of the great disservices society has wrought on my brothers is teaching them to fear certain "feminine" traits. Jeffery M. Smith refers to this phenomenon as "fear of femininity."[18] Such fear can manifest itself in the following ways:

▪ Restrictive emotionality
▪ Socialized control, power, and competition
▪ Homophobia
▪ Restrictive sexual and affectionate behavior
▪ Obsession with achievement and success
▪ Health problems

While some of this may very well be true, when counselors are competent, nonjudgmental, culturally responsive, and discerning, they can overcome some of the challenges named by Black men for avoiding therapy. While a lot of time is spent discussing these challenges, not enough is spent on the impact of clinicians' biases and negative perceptions of Black men on counseling outcomes. And, let's face it, many if not most Black men have not had positive experiences with institutional powers—the public school system, law enforcement agencies, the courts, health care facilities, to name a few. We have more than enough reasons to be leery of power structures that have historically been the sources of our suffering. We Black men must change, too. We must learn to seek help when we are not well. We must learn the language of self-care by reaching out beyond toxic masculinity and relentless patriarchy.

In thinking about ways counselors and other mental health professionals sometimes oppress clients, author Ivory Toldson list fives traps that counselors fall prey to:

1. *Using biased psychological tests to inform counseling decisions.* As a social work instructor at Fordham University and Lehman College, I spend a healthy amount of time speaking to my students about the need to take assessment instruments with a grain of salt. I often tell them that no single instrument is comprehensive enough to tell them all they need to know about a client. Additionally, the best experts about my brothers' lives are my brothers themselves. In other words, we are the owners of our stories, and, as such, clinicians should partner *with us* in learning *about us*. Assessments are valuable tools to inform counseling, but they are not the final arbiters of who the client is or what that person needs. For example, a clinician assessing why a 27-year-old young man still lives with his elderly grandmother might conclude that there is some dependency and enmeshment present in the relationship. Such as assessment would obviously lack cultural responsiveness. We know that within the African American construction of family, systems of support often run to three to four generations deep.

2. *Writing or endorsing reports that emphasize deficits.* I was a school social worker for many years and an assistant principal for almost four years. During that time, I saw more than a few reports about students who used deficit language and exaggerated alleged incidents they might have been involved in or infractions they may have committed. I often tell emerging clinicians to seriously consider meeting clients before reading reports about them in order to get an authentic view of the client before drawing conclusions. The deficit or medical model in mental health counseling has long been proven to be ineffective. The medical model can be understood as a treatment approach that seeks and treats disease. It is called the deficit model because the primary aim is to find, diagnose, and treat illnesses. It does not name or celebrate health and wholeness. People are motivated to do and be better when they are celebrated, not chastised. As the song goes, "Be patient with me. God is not through with me yet."[19] A strength-based approach to counseling, on the other hand, looks for ways to leverage people's gifts, talents, community, relationships, grit, and the ability to bounce back from adversity. We know that people tend to do better when we start from a place of strength.

3. *Endorsing the use of psychotropic medication to suppress culturally or developmentally appropriate behaviors.* Schools have a long history of overmedicating young Black young men due to the ridiculous fear that they cannot be controlled. This is yet another social and emotional tool used by society to break our individuality and personality. In most traditional schools, students are expected to remain in their seats for much of the day. If they get up too often, they are placed on that dreaded IEP list. When I was starting my career in social work, I worked for a not-for-profit organization that served young men of color. I recall a conversation I had with a young African American client about what it was like to be prescribed psychotropic medication. He said that while his teachers and mother preferred the medicated version of himself, he felt like he was having an out-of-body experience. He said he did not feel his rhythm. While he agreed that he got into less trouble while on medication, he felt isolated from his authentic self. Please don't misunderstand me. I am not anti-medication. Rather, I am for exploring holistic and natural ways of coping with both our inner and outer lived experiences. This may or may not include psychotropic medication. For example, natural remedies such as St. John's Wort, bright light therapy, acupuncture, exercise, mindfulness-based therapy (MBT), problem-solving therapy (PST), and omega-3 fatty acids have all been proven to remedy major depressive disorder.[20] We also know that people are at their best when they are connected to the community. Human connection is one of the most profound and enduring antidotes against isolation and alienation.

4. *Using the majority culture as the basis for behavioral norms.* The Black man who seeks counseling often does so due to the issues he faces living in a society that has labeled him a menace. Some of those issues that brings him to counseling might include court mandated interventions, suicidal ideation and attempts, family conflict, persistent trauma that intersects with poverty and racism. Inevitably, those compounding issues have a deleterious effect on our familial and intimate relationships. We are reminded daily on Fox News, in the movies, and in our daily interactions with the world that our ways of sitting on the margins of the acceptable norm. That is, we don't quite fit in. Our tone when speaking is interpreted as that of an "angry Black man." Our scholarship and brilliance are often delegated as belonging to another group, "You are acting White." We express ourselves the way we know how, and such creativity and individuality are interpreted as "gangster behaviors." When we give in to the demand to conform, we are accused of acting White. This is especially true for Black professionals who find themselves

homeless because they are not accepted by the dominant culture on one hand and are accused of being a "sell out" by their community of origin. Counselors can support Black men by seeing them as experts in their own lives. They should be attentive to the goals and dreams of those who come to them for support. They should not rush to prescribed behavioral norms but allow clients to reimagine their own stories. They *should*: Ask more questions, listen, remain curious and inquisitive about the client's worldviews and aspirations. They *should*: Set goals that are co-constructed with the client and respect him enough to share the power in the counseling space. They *should*: Validate both his experiences and his worldview while challenging him to explore the boundaries of his fullest human potential.

5. *Adhering to a diagnostic classification system without regard for cultural considerations.* Colmore and Moore remind us why so many people, including significant others, complain about why Black men avoid sharing their inner feelings. According to the authors, such reluctance to self-disclose in counseling and beyond is rooted in the history of slavery. They note, "During slavery, African American men were often forbidden to exercise certain freedoms (e.g., freedom of speech, the right to vote, etc.), which were granted to European American men. Those who chose not to follow protocol or abide by the rules suffered severe and unpleasant consequences." The authors further note that some men are leery of the "magical power" of counseling to manipulate and control their minds.[21] The way to combat these ingrained suspicions is by establishing trust and building a positive, healthy client–counselor relationship. According to Madison-Colmore and Moore, the cultural divide many men of color experience in counseling can often be overcome if counselors:

   a. Carefully assess their own belief system.
   b. Develop a positive therapeutic relationship with the client.
   c. Address the client's unique experiences (e.g., racism and discrimination).
   d. Identify the client's specific needs.
   e. Assist the client in assessing his own lifestyle.

A Promising Model for Therapy with Black Men

The recently departed bell hooks reminded us about what is often ignored about men and our emotions. She said that, after signing up for counseling:

It was hard for me to face that I did not want to hear about his feelings when they were painful or negative, that I did not want my image of the strong man truly challenged by learning of his weaknesses and vulnerabilities. Here I was, an enlightened feminist woman who did not want to hear my man speak his pain because it revealed his emotional vulnerabilities.[22]

It's not that men hide emotion; it is that the world only recognizes particular expressions of our emotions. Her observation that anger is the best concealment of pain and anguish is more than a little astute. Anger masks the pain for both the person expressing it and the person it's directed at. Too often, misunderstood rage closes the door to better relationships, better mental health, and a brighter future.

Before offering a model of treatment for Black men, it is worth noting that the research is clear. "African Americans preferred to work with Black psychologists due to an assumption of shared racial and cultural understanding that White American psychologists may not possess. The desire for a racially similar and culturally attuned psychotherapist may be a more salient concern for Black male clients."[23] And, why wouldn't or shouldn't it be so? We all want to engage in vulnerable conversations with people that understand and have experienced our suffering. The client shouldn't have to spend half of the session explaining what it feels like to be followed around a department store to a clinician who has never experienced this. We must encourage more Black men to become clinicians. Recent data shows that "at the graduate level, Black men make up approximately 2 percent of all graduate students in psychology and only 1 percent of all graduate students in clinical psychology."[24] According to Beasley, Miller, and Cokely, the numbers are even more dismal at the doctoral level with Black men earning 1 percent of all doctoral degrees earned in the same field.

It's important to note that a counselor who looks and speaks like the client is not a guarantee of a successful outcome. This is a triggering point for me because when the opposite is true, very few questions are raised. No one bats an eye when a staff of predominantly White teachers is teaching in a school that comprises predominantly Black and Brown children. Few raise questions about culturally responsive teachers and learning or, in this case, counseling. But, the minute we call for more men of color to work with Black boys and men, the question of competence over color and gender is brought into focus. To those critics, I say I want both. I want competent Black men working with men and boys to address issues unique to Black men and boys. To those critics, I say return to the data of why men and boys often refuse counseling services. Return to the fact that Black men make up between 1 and 2 percent of those receiving advanced degrees in clinical psychology. That alone is evidence of the uphill battle Black men and boys in America face.

H.I.S. Counseling Model with African American Men

Octavia Madison-Colmore of Virginia Polytechnic Institute and State University and James Moore III of University of South Carolina propose a three-step approach to working with Black men that speaks to our unique historical and cultural experiences in the United States. Untested empirically, the model borrows from the bio-psychosocial and affirmation approaches to psychotherapy. H.I.S. stands for History, Identity, and Spirituality. The authors make the case that any meaningful work with African American men rests on a clear understanding of our culture, history, and experiences. I have been training and mentoring clinicians at the graduate and doctoral levels for the last 15 years. One of the things that I teach my students is that of all the tools that they will bring to the therapeutic space, the most important will be themselves. Black men want to be seen for who *they* are, not for what society says about them. They want to know that their clinician withholds judgment and stereotypes and is willing and able to hear, hold, and honor the stories they tell. Speaking specifically on this, the authors note that it is a good idea to have the client do a *cultural genogram*. One of my colleagues at Fordham University, Elaine Congress, developed the cultural genogram. Similar to a traditional genogram, a culture genogram (or culturegram) gathers information about the basic structure of a person's family, his demographic, functioning level, and the relationships between members of his family of origin. However, the culturegram takes this process a step further, including extended and unrelated family members (e.g., friends, neighbors, church members).[25] I don't mean to imply that White clinicians are not able to listen, learn, and develop the empathetic skills to support African American men in counseling. What I am saying is that African American men need healers that understand and have themselves experienced similar racial discrimination.

The second step in the H.I.S. model is *identity*. How does one develop a healthy identity in the face of 400 years of oppression and marginalization? The counseling space cannot only become what Christopher Lasch calls a "haven of rest"[26] from a cruel world; it can also become a space where Black men are safe to rewrite their stories—stories that can then be taken into the workplace, marketplace, the highways and byways of this world and spoken with pride and confidence.

By inviting Black men to look beyond a long and painful history of oppression to their rich and sometimes hidden heritage, the counseling space can become a place of rebirth and healing. In protecting my very soul against a relentless narrative "to know and stay in my subordinate place," I constantly scour the history of my people so that I may claim their blood and brilliance as mine. Yes, I lay a firm claim to Bob Marley and Marcus Garvey and Harry Belafonte, my Jamaican brothers. James Baldwin, Langston Hughes, Frederick Douglas—they all belong to me, too, and I to them. I claim the prophetic voice of Martin Luther King Jr. and the brilliance of Muhammad Ali. I claim Thurgood Marshall, W. E. B. Du Bois, Aaron Douglas, and all of my unknown ancestors on whose shoulders I stand. They are all mine. Sankofa tells me to go back and retrieve that which is at risk of being left behind. I reclaim my ancestral brilliance and beauty in the face of a world that would crush my light and life. Needless to say, I would not dare leave behind Sojourner Truth, Nanny the Maroon, Harriet Tubman, and my beloved mother, Merica Ball, and so many more. I claim them all.

I am also intentional in connecting with other Black men who provide me with informal therapeutic, social, moral, and spiritual support, and I them. One such group I belong to is called Raising Black Men. In it, we mentor young men and each other into developing healthy identities and wholeness.[27] When counseling Black men, it is critical to remember that the therapeutic is not owned by the therapist. Pastors, professors, community leaders, barbers, and other informal relationships can be invaluable to identity formation for African American men. The counselor can serve as a sort of shepherd-shaman or historian in helping Black men to reclaim identities that they can be proud of. Renowned scholar and educator on racism in education, Beverly Daniel Tatum, said that "joining with one's peers for support in the face of stress is a positive coping strategy. What is problematic is that the young people are operating with very limited definitions of what it means to be Black, based largely on cultural stereotypes."[28] Dr. Samuel Woodard advances a group process with young men using the "seven traditional African values: (a) respect, (b) responsibility, (c) reciprocity (good deeds come back to you), (d) restraint (the group before selfish needs), (e) reason (resolving disputes through the group), (f) reconciliation (forgiveness), and (g) reverence (homage to the Creator)."[29] At its best, the counseling space can be a place of healing, empowerment, and reclamation for Black men of all ages. But, this must start with clinicians who know our history and see the value in identity reformation.

Spirituality is the final step in the H.I.S. counseling model. Madison-Colmore and Moore submit that, within the African American tradition, spirituality is generally associated with the church. That might be so for older generations. Today, however, many young men and women find solace and spiritual fulfillment outside of traditional faith communities. On the other hand, the Black church has long been a refuge for African American men. Six out of seven days, we are ignored, demeaned, and treated like second-class citizens. But, at church on Sunday, we find not just belonging but respect. On Sunday, we get to testify. On Sunday, we get to share our stories, sing our songs, play our music, confess our sins, celebrate our accomplishments, break communal bread, and simply breathe before reentering a hostile world on Monday morning. The issue of spirituality and Black men will be dealt with in greater detail in the culminating chapter of this book. But, on the issue of mental health and spirituality, Black men often are more trusting of their ministers and thus are more likely to seek spiritual and mental health support from them. This is one of the reasons faith leaders should be trained in basic counseling theories and techniques. Part of this training should also be knowing the boundaries of one's expertise and when to refer out for more targeted support such as physical or psychiatric care.

Making Mental Health Treatment More Accessible

We have all been there. We have all been waitlisted to get into our favorite restaurant or to get on that last flight heading home. But, as inconvenient as these aggravations are, neither compares to being waitlisted to see a doctor when facing a mental health crisis. One of the things we know about crisis management is that systems that are already stretched thin will buckle under the pressures of additional stressors. This is definitely true of our current health care system. The story of Daniel Prude is not an uncommon one. Many men and women as well as young people are discharged from emergency rooms with referral lists that are, in many cases, outdated. When they call those community clinics and agencies, they hear things like:

- The clinic is no longer accepting new patients at this time.
- We do not accept your insurance.
- The next available appointment is three to four months out.

These hospitals do not have enough beds. Consequently, far too many people with serious mental health struggles who should be hospitalized in order to receive proper treatment and medication are sent back into the community where the infrastructure to support them are themselves at their breaking point. Insurance companies are telling clients that they just have to keep calling the next facility on their list until they get one that is accepting new patients. This says nothing about other the variables and services including faith-based counseling, therapists within one's geographical community, tele-therapy for those who need it, therapists of color, and/or the need for clinicians that specialize certain areas like sexual violence and substance abuse.

Conclusion

The issue of mental health care for Black men is complex because it intersects with gender, race, culture, socioeconomics, and parity. In this chapter, I outlined why mental health care must be more readily available to Black men. Black men are at the greatest risk for poverty, unemployment, incarceration, exposure to violence, and early death. There's much work to be done so that the next Daniel Prude does not end up dead at the hands of those who are charged to serve and protect. There is much work to be done so that those who report to hospitals because they are having a mental health crisis are not turned away. Yes, there needs to be work around expanding insurance and community access, not just for intervention but for preventative care as well. While it's easy to focus on the individual needs through a deficit lens, it's more important to raise serious questions about systemic issues that starve people of color, in this case Black men, of the services they need.

Additionally, there is much work that schools, faith communities, the media, and other community organizations need to do to de-stigmatize mental illness. Too many members of our community continue to suffer needlessly. Awareness is the first step in this process. This awareness should remove the shame and stigma that continues to surround treatment. It should also educate the general population about the treatment options available to those suffering from various forms of mental health conditions. With all the social, economic, and communal barriers that we face, access to quality mental health services is crucial. It is indeed one of the pressing issues of our time that must be addressed—at all levels of society.

Notes

1. Wizdom Powell Hammond, "Taking It Like a Man: Masculine Role Norms as Moderators of the Racial Discrimination–Depressive Symptoms Association Among African American Men," *American Journal of Public Health* 102, no. S2 (2012): S232–S241.
2. Benita N. Chatmon, "Males and Mental Health Stigma," *American Journal of Men's Health* 14, no. 4 (2020).

3. Sidney H. Hankerson, Derek Suite, and Rahn K. Bailey, "Treatment Disparities among African American Men Are with Depression: Implications for Clinical Practice," *Journal of Health Care for the Poor and Underserved* 26, no. 1 (2015): 21.

4. Nancy Schimelpfening, "Differences in Suicide Among Men and Women," Very Well Mind (2011), https://www.verywellmind.com/gender-differences-in-suicide-methods-1067508.

5. Vincent J. Felitti, Robert F. Anda, Dale Nordenberg, David F. Williamson, Alison M. Spitz, Valerie Edwards, and James S. Marks, "Relationship of Childhood Abuse and Household Dysfunction to Many of the Leading Causes of Death in Adults: The Adverse Childhood Experiences (ACE) Study," *American Journal of Preventive Medicine* 14, no. 4 (1998): 245–258.

6. https://www.barewellgroup.com/blog/black-history-mental-health

7. Greer, Tawanda M., and Klaus E. Cavalhieri. "The role of coping strategies in understanding the effects of institutional racism on mental health outcomes for African American men." *Journal of Black Psychology* 45(5) (2019): 405–433. (quote is on 408)

8. Van der Kolk, Bessel. "The body keeps the score: Brain, mind, and body in the healing of trauma." New York (2014).

9. Greer & Cavalhieri, Op. Cit.

10. Doris A. Fuller, H. Richard Lamb, Michael Biasotti, and John Snook, "Overlooked in the Undercounted: The Role of Mental Illness in Fatal Law Enforcement Encounters," Treatment Advocacy Center (2015).

11. Stephen J. Blumberg, Tainya C. Clarke, and Debra L. Blackwell, "Racial and Ethnic Disparities in Men's Use of Mental Health Treatments," US CDC, National Center For Health Statistics, 2015.

12. "What Is Mental Health Parity?" NAMI, accessed August 28, 2022, https://www.nami.org/Your-Journey/Individuals-with-Mental-Illness/Understanding-Health-Insurance/What-is-Mental-Health-Parity.

13. Brian Levack, "The Horrors of Witchcraft and Demonic Possession," *Social Research* 81, no. 4 (2014): 921–939.

14. Shawn O. Utsey, "Racism and the Psychological Well-Being of African American Men," *Journal of African American Men* (1997): 69–87.

15. Brian L. Ragsdale, "Surveillance of African American Men and Its Possible Effect on Social, Emotional, and Psychological Functioning," *Journal of African American Men* 5, no. 1 (2000): 33–42.

16. Julie A. Flanagan, "Restricting Electronic Monitoring in the Private Workplace," *Duke Library Journal* 43 (1993): 1256.

17. Karen Barone, "Barriers among Men Seeking Mental Health Services," *Electronic Theses, Projects, and Dissertations* 1380 (2022).

18. Jeffrey M. Smith, "Fear as a Barrier: African American Men's Avoidance of Counseling Services," *Journal of African American Men* 6, no. 4 (2002): 47–60.

19. Albertina Walker and James *Cleveland, Please Be Patient With Me,* YouTube.

20. Marlene P. Freeman, Maurizio Fava, James Lake, Madhukar H. Trivedi, Katherine L. Wisner, and David Mischoulon, "Complementary and Alternative Medicine in Major Depressive Disorder: The American Psychiatric Association Task Force Report," *Journal of Clinical Psychiatry* 71, no. 6 (2010): 669.

21. Octavia Madison-Colmore and James L. Moore III, "Using the HIS Model in Counseling African-American Men," *The Journal of Men's Studies* 10, no. 2 (2002): 197–208.

22. bell hooks, *The Will to Change: Men, Masculinity, and Love, Beyond Words* (Atria Books, 2004).

23. Samuel T. Beasley, IS Keino Miller, and Kevin O. Cokley, "Exploring the Impact of Increasing the Number of Black Men in Professional Psychology," *Journal of Black Studies* 46, no. 7 (2015): 704–722.

24. Ibid, p. 705.

25. Madison-Colmore and Moore III, "Using the HIS Model..."

26. Christopher Lasch, *Haven in a Heartless World: The Family Besieged* (WW Norton & Company, 1995).

27. Smith, "Fear as a Barrier ..."

28. Keyiona Ritchey, "Black Identity Development," *The Vermont Connection* 35, no. 1 (2014): 12.

29. Frederick D. Harper, Linda M. Terry, and Rashida Twiggs. "Counseling Strategies with Black Boys and Black Men: Implications for Policy," *The Journal of Negro Education* (2009): 216–232.

5

Learning to Love Other People's Children

Black and Brown children aren't stupid. They know when they aren't being treated like White children. They sense when they are welcome in a classroom versus when they are merely tolerated. Much of this chapter will explore the need for inclusivity in the curriculum, the overrepresentation of young men of color in special education classrooms, and the suspension and expulsion rate of Black and Brown adolescent males. Before diving in, however, I want to ask a question that will, I hope, anchor the chapter.

What if loving other people's children was a prerequisite for teaching them?

What if teachers were required to love other people's children the way they would their own? Na'llah Suah Nasir and colleagues, in their book, *We Dare to Say Love*, note, "Society and the schools embedded within it have made love a foreign thing for Black males." They continue, "It has become difficult to comprehend a sincere relationship between public schools and Black male students (or all Black children for that matter) that is predicated on love."[1] They are correct. Our first order of business is to love

---

No Country For Black Men, pages 69–88
Copyright © 2023 by Information Age Publishing
www.infoagepub.com
69

the children we are asked to teach. Imagine spending most of your waking hours with people that you know do not love, or even like, you, people who have low expectations of you and for you, people who are constantly throwing you out of the classroom—essentially throwing you away. Imagine having to enter such hostile environments year after year. Imagine your first-grade teacher forming a narrative about who you and your family are, only to pass on that same narrative to your second grade teacher, and so on up through high school.

Learning to love other people's children is a moral imperative. As long as teachers continue to see Black children as mere extensions of the building they work in, they will never love them. As long as Black children's abilities, culture, and color are measured through a colonial lens, they will never feel the love of their teachers. Learning to love other people's children is also a policy imperative. When teachers remain emotionally distant from students of color, when they treat them as inconveniences, as something to be borne, not cherished, when they cannot see past their prejudices, they are cultivating an environment that is as toxic as it is oppressive. In such an unwelcoming environment, academic expectations are lowered and intolerance for students sends them to suspension rooms thus perpetuating the school to prison pipeline so many young Black men find themselves traveling. In the opinion piece, "Students Learn from People They Love," David Brook of the *New York Times* notes:

> The early neuroscience breakthrough reminded us that a key job of a school is to give students new things to love—an exciting field of study, new friends...it reminded us that what teachers really teach is themselves—their contagious passion for their subjects and students.[2]

In order for teachers to be effective, they must offer their lives and the lives of their students as integral parts of the curriculum. In the words of Zaretta Hammond, "One of the goals of education is not simply to fill students with facts and information but to help them learn how to learn."[3] Learning how to learn creates transferable and transformative learning that is strong enough to greet both obstacles and opportunities throughout their lives. That is what my mother would call a "good education."

When he was in the first grade, my son, Michael—whose picture is on the cover of this book—was accepted into a gifted and talented program. At a parent teacher meeting early in the semester, we were informed that Michael was a bit antisocial. He often sat alone and did not engage with other students. The teacher told us that he did not speak much and seemed withdrawn and apathetic. I was jolted by her perception of my child. I proceeded to ask her what she did to include him in the classroom community. She didn't do anything. I asked her if she spent any time speaking with him alone. She did not. I asked her if she reached out to his mother or me to see how she could engage him. Again, she did not. This school was much larger than the one our son previously attended. It was unfamiliar, and my son likely felt some measure of anxiety. While it's true that Michael was a relatively taciturn child, he did speak with a little encouragement. I couldn't understand how it was that this White teacher could not understand: (a) the developmental needs and opportunities of a six-year-old boy or (b) the common-sense practice of welcoming a new student into the school community. That encounter was the first of a string of similar incidents that occurred throughout Michael's education and continue to occur today. Ibram X. Kendi, in his book, *Stamped from the Beginning: The Definitive History of Racist Ideas in America,* narrates the history of racist ideas "from their origins in fifteenth-century Europe, through colonial times when the early British settlers carried racist ideas to America, all the way to the twenty-first century and current debates about the events taking place in our streets"[4]—and classrooms, I would add. This teacher, however good her intentions, had branded my son from the beginning. His silence was pathologized in this new environment. We had high hopes that this school would equip my son with the tools to maximize his human potential. Sadly, we soon learned that the opposite was true. In this chapter, I will name some of the obstacles that young Black males face at all levels of their educational journey, from grade school to university.

They Are Just Different From Us: Outgroup Homogeneity

The social and behavioral sciences have long raised questions about how *ingroup favoritism* shows up in our ordinary interactions with members of our own group. These sciences have also raised questions about the causes and consequences of *outgroup derogation,* discriminating against the outgroup. Examples of outgroup derogation include treating the outgroup with hostility, making negative evaluations about the outgroup, attributing negative traits and responsibility for negative incidents to outgroup members.[5] Everett and colleagues observe:

> It is in our group-based character that the angels and demons of human nature can be seen: on the one hand, the success of intragroup cooperation that has given us democracy and civil rights; and on the other hand, the darkness of intergroup conflict that has given us the collective stains on human history of genocide and war.[6]

Whether we look at ingroup favoritism and outgroup[7] derogation through implicit bias theory or through some other evolutionary survival lens such as conflict or scarcity theories, we do know that educators who see the children they are educating as outgroups often treat them unjustly. So, how do we get school personnel to love other people's children when they see those children as other? Othering students leads to fear, misunderstanding, and ultimately to miseducation and mistreatment. I have seen teachers, clinicians, and other prospective employees turn down job opportunities in urban school communities out of genuine fear of the neighborhoods these schools service and the children who reside in them. This fear should never be underestimated because it cultivates cruelty and isolation and diminishes the object of said fear. I have had too many conversations with young White educators who admit that they struggle to connect with students not only because they do not understand their culture, but because they are afraid of Black and Brown children. How can you teach, much less love, other people's children when you are afraid of them? You can't create and nurture an educational haven for children if you fear them. Betina Love, writing an opinion piece for *Education Week*, argues, "White teachers need to *want* to address how they contribute to structural racism. They need to join the fight for education justice, racial justice, housing justice, immigration justice, food justice, queer and trans justice, labor justice, and, above all, the fight for humanity."[8] The process of teaching and learning must operationalize and integrate students' lived experiences with love. White (especially female) teachers can't enter the Black space without first addressing the issues faced by Black students. Those teachers must be willing to examine how their own fear, hostility, and indifference towards students of color perpetuates a culture of oppression. They then need to join the fight to end structural racism in our schools.

A study done in the Denver County Public School District on the experiences of African American students, teachers, and administrators reveals what we have long known: Black children are punished more harshly and are treated differently from their White counterparts. Chalkbeat, a nonprofit news organization that covers education in American communities, highlights this deplorable treatment of Black students by punctuating this difference:

> Two teachers from an unnamed school discussed the respective outcomes for two students, one Black and one white. The white student, who threw chairs around the classroom, was promoted to a higher math class after someone deemed his actions the result of being bored in class. The Black student, who simply balled his fists, was suspended.[9]

In the next section, I will show that the issue of punishing Black and Brown youth is not about the behaviors of our young men but the misuse of power by educational institutions that are still steeped in White supremacy. Black parents have mastered the jargon of attempting to keep our children safe outside of our homes. We teach them how to respond to the police when pulled over. "Hands on the wheel. Don't talk back to the police in a disrespectful way. Say what you're doing when reaching for your license and registration." They know what to do when they are called into the principal's office for horseplay. "Ask to call your mother or father. Ask to go to your favorite teacher's room to take a break or calm down rather than going back and forth with that male teacher who triggers you." Because we feel helpless against the school system, we control what we can—our children. Yet, even when we teach them how to respond, they still get suspended. They still get expelled. They are still placed in the detention room. They are still asked to leave the classroom. They still die in police custody.

Segregation in Plain Sight: Eyes to See but Cannot See

If you were to ask ten White people what they think of when they hear the word "segregation," most of them will reference images from the 1960s: the ubiquitous "Whites only" signs hanging on store entrances, Plessy v. Ferguson, Rosa Parks. And, if you were to ask those same people how those images change if you add the word "education," it's a safe bet you'd hear answers like, Brown vs. The Board of Education, George Wallace facing off against Vivian Malone, the Chester school protests. But, segregation, unfortunately, is not a phenomenon relegated to the tomes of history, the unsavory byproduct of a less enlightened society. Oh, I know there are no more colored drinking fountains. Black and White people share the same lavatories, eat in the same restaurants, shop at the same supermarkets. Black children and White children ride the same buses to school, attend the same classes, change for physical education in the same locker rooms. Just because something isn't overt, though, doesn't mean it doesn't exist. While many may believe that the era of segregation is a thing of the past, the truth is, in many ways, America is still segregated. We are segregated in our weekend worship, by our zip codes, by our socioeconomic status, by our body politic, by our gender, by our skin color. Our education system is no exception in this segregated America.

A few years ago, I attended a meeting at my son's high school. The superintendent gave his remarks and then opened the floor for a question-and-answer session. A middle-aged White woman stood up in a library that was filled with people of different ethnicities and launched into a tirade about how it was not fair for the children of taxpayers who lived on "this side of the city" to be sent to school on the south side. She insisted that "these children, our children should be given preferred seats in schools over here." She said that the children on the south side should be placed in their own schools down there. I could not believe what I was hearing. The words of George Wallace rang out in my mind: "Segregation now, segregation tomorrow and segregation forever." Unable to stomach this woman's gall, I rose to my feet and said something to the effect of, "You realize that this city was one of the last cities to attempt to desegregate its schools? You realize that you are advocating segregation?" I decided that since I went that far, I might as well go a bit further. I proceeded to name the schools that are designated for the "gifted and talented" and how those schools have not served Black and Brown children or immigrant families well. I told her that we need to further desegregate our schools not to return to the past. I sat down with an indignant thud. Many in that packed library stood up and applauded including the superintendent.

At its core, White supremacy espouses domination. It assumes that its ideology is superior to all others. That entitled White woman believed that for her anointed White children, attending the "better schools" was their right. For everyone else, it was an inconvenient privilege. This woman's shriveled heart was beating with love for her own children, but she had not been taught how to love other people's. In the next two sections, I will describe how special education designation, as well as the use of harsh disciplinary measures, has been used to segregate, miseducate, and traumatize young men of color.

The Overrepresentation of Black Boys in Special Education

For most young men of color living in urban communities, a special education designation is an academic death sentence. Even though there is solid evidence that special education curricula have not served our young men well, we still blindly place them in those programs and classrooms. Special education designation is no panacea, nor will it ever be because the very root of how young men get it is rotten. When teachers are frustrated with students' lack of academic progress, instead of assessing their own teaching methodologies, they ask that students be assessed for special education services. (Many parent–teacher meetings lead off with, "I am no psychologist, but I am sure he has some form of intellectual disability.") When they are angry and frustrated with behavioral noncompliance, instead of evaluating if their perception of Black students is tinged with their White supremacy, they ask that these boys be screened for emotional disturbance. ("I'm not a clinician, but I am sure he has oppositional defiant disorder.") Hani Morgan notes:

> Low-income students are more often identified in subjective disability categories, such as emotional disability and intellectual disability, and more frequently placed in separate classrooms. Further, after being identified in this manner, these pupils tend to be placed in classrooms where academic outcomes are worse, expectations for success are lower, and the stigma associated with special education is higher. They are also frequently placed in classrooms with teachers who have less expertise in math, English, and science. These circumstances have raised concerns about systemic racial bias because low-income children are more likely to be students of color.[10]

"Children are suffering from a toxic cocktail of poverty, illiteracy, racial discrimination and massive incarceration that sentences poor boys to dead-end and hopeless lives," notes Marian Wright Edelman, onetime president of the Children's Defense Fund.[11] The miseducation of African American males in the United States is one of, if not the most pressing crises in public school education today. We hear a lot of talk about preparing students to compete in a 21st century global marketplace. What we don't hear is the subversive crisis that continues to leave young men of color behind. A decade ago, a dismal 12 percent of Black fourth-grade males were proficient in reading, compared to 38 percent of White males. Mathematics performance showed an almost identical statistic (12 percent proficiency for Black boys, 44 percent for White).[12] Those numbers are more dismal when looking at data of districts and of urban communities.

The disproportionate number of African American males in special education programs is all the evidence we need that racism is alive and well. More than any other demographic, Black male students are given subjective and artificial labels that stymy and diminish their human possibilities. Labels such as emotionally disturbed, attention deficit hyperactivity, and oppositional defiant disorder legitimize the reason these students are segregated. Additionally, as indicated earlier, they are then placed in classrooms with the least qualified teachers. They are also suspended more than any other group. This is the stubborn and persistent legacy of racism in the United States. This is why Black men continue to struggle for a piece of the American dream. We have no country.

Black Boys and the "Emotionally Disturbed" Label

For the 2018–2019 academic year, 10,262 public school students were classified as emotionally disturbed—5,040 were Black. The gender distribution was significant as well, with a ratio of approximately 4:1 (7,728 male; 2,534 female). Of the nearly 8,000 boys, the majority were African American.[13] Under the Individuals with Disabilities Act (IDEA), to qualify for special education, students must have a disability that falls under one of the 13 categories, emotional disturbance being one of them. Recently, the New York Department of Education has made it a priority to reimagine a label for students who struggle to regulate their emotions or who have some form of diagnosed psychological or emotional disability.[14] IDEA defines emotional disturbance as:

- an inability to learn that cannot be explained by intellectual, sensory, or health factors;
- an inability to build or maintain interpersonal relationships with peers and teachers;
- inappropriate types of behavior or feelings in average or unremarkable situations;
- a general pervasive mood of unhappiness or depression; and
- a tendency to develop symptoms or fears associated with personal or school-related problems.

Moniqueka Gold and Heraldo Richards, in their article, "To Label or Not to Label: The Special Education Question for African Americans," argue:

> The process of labeling affects both the persons doing the labeling (the labeler) and the persons labeled (the labeled). The labelers, members of the majority (e.g., European Americans), are subject to biases (preferences), prejudices (prejudgments; decisions based on limited or inaccurate information), and stereotypes (overgeneralization).[15]

The authors should have made clear that it is the labeled children and their futures who are affected by such labels, not the labelers. The power resides with the labelers—power to isolate children from their community and peers, to narrow the academic and economic futures of the labeled children, to sentence students to being labeled for the rest of their lives.

Suspension and the Criminalization of Black Boys

I am always fascinated with how schools gravitate to the latest curriculum on social and emotional learning that offers new techniques and theories that promise maximum compliance from children. Go into just about any classroom and you will see all sorts of charts, creeds, and PBIS matrices from the RULER program that attempts to teach children to regulate their emotions to Lee Canter's Assertive Discipline to the Multi-Tiered System of Support (MTSS). Schools relish diving into the theoretical underpinnings of such programs and spend tens of thousands of dollars implementing them in their schools. The latest "miraculous" curriculum promises fantastical results—compliance, improved academic performance, willing and eager students who ask, "How high" when the teacher says, "Jump." Educators have convinced themselves that the right curriculum will create these Stepford students who color inside the lines and happily do as they're told. When these programs inevitably fail to deliver, blame falls on the "irredeemable," "irremediable" students, not on a faulty curriculum, never on teacher bias, never on an institution infected with racism.

I have seen it far too many times. We are always ready to unpack curricula that lack the teeth to address the real issues in public education. The irony with the RULER program—created by an organization that is built on taking care of people and their emotional well-being—that is so popular in urban schools is that recently—one of their key African American Staff and scholars made a very public break from the program because of discriminatory practices that made it impossible for them to remain there. One of the hardest things for White school systems to do is face their White rage and its impact on Black and Brown students and people as a whole. In fact, Carol Anderson, the author of *White Rage,* notes:

> White rage is not about visible violence, but rather it works its way through the courts, the legislatures, and a range of government bureaucracies. It wreaks havoc subtly, almost imperceptibly. Too imperceptibly, certainly, for a nation consistently drawn to the spectacular—to what it can see. It's not the Klan. White rage doesn't have to wear sheets, burn crosses, or take to the streets. Working the halls of power, it can achieve its ends far more effectively, far more destructively.[16]

Though Anderson's point is well taken, most of us would object to the assertion that "White rage is not about the violence." Not ten days ago, in fact, on May 14, ten people were killed and three more were wounded when a man opened fire at a supermarket in Buffalo, New York. Eighteen-year-old Peyton S. Gendron drove two hours to a supermarket that was frequented primarily by African Americans. With the N-word sketched into his AR-15, he methodically killed ten African Americans and injured three. Ms. Anderson is wrong. White rage kills.

If "no compelling research studies support the claim that African American boys are more disruptive than their peers" then why do they continue to be suspended at such a young age at such inordinate rates?[17] Consider making sense of this data point from the U.S. Department of Education: "While 6 percent of all K–12 students received one or more out of school suspensions [in 2016], the percentage is 18 percent for black boys; 10 percent for black girls; 5 percent for white boys; and 2 percent for white girls."[18] Why do you think Black boys are suspended four times the rate of White boys? Why do you think Black girls are suspended four times the rate of White girls? Educators fault poverty, fatherless homes, ghetto culture, and maladaptive behaviors for why school officials have to employ draconian disciplinary measures to "fix" Black students. It's easier to point the finger at the child than confront their own racist ideologies and discriminatory behaviors. Russell J. Skiba and Natasha T. Williams, educators from Indiana State University who spearheaded The Equity Project, note, "The crux of the matter then is whether Black students engage in more seriously disruptive behaviors that could justify different rates and severity of consequences." Though many have attempted to find evidentiary support that would prove this hypothesis true, they always come up empty handed. There is "little to no evidence that African American students in the same school or district are engaging in more seriously disruptive behavior that could warrant higher rates of exclusion or punishment."[19] If Black boys and girls are not exhibiting more egregious behaviors than their White counterparts, then why are they being suspended at such an alarmingly higher rate? As tempting as it might be to refute the data that Black kids are no worse than others to justify harsher punishment, the truth is that the punishment is not a reflection of our children but of the punishers.

Employing a zero-tolerance policy in schools that are supposed to teach children how to become productive citizens is foolish. This simply does not work with children. Imagine if we employed such policies in our families, communities, or places of work? Every infraction would be cause to terminate marriages, employees, friendships, and the like. Better yet, imagine a zero-tolerance policy from the Divine One? We would all make our beds in hell. Zero tolerance says nothing about our Black and Brown children and everything about what those of us in power think about them. Alice Darensbourg, an expert who has studied issues educational disparity among Black and LatinX students, argues:

> The rigidity used when enforcing zero tolerance policies may affect African American males at higher rates due to the way they are viewed by school staff, their evidence of higher office referral rates, and the disproportionate allocation of exclusionary discipline they receive from their districts.[20]

There's a saying: "When all you have is a hammer, everything looks like a nail." The same is true when we see Black and Brown children as problems to be solved. Whether we're aware of it or not, we adopt a hostile orientation towards them. As such, minor infractions receive major punishments. It's the same principle that dragged Emmitt Till out of his bed and left him at the bottom of the Tallahatchie River. Punishments are representative of the punisher, not the punished. Black and Brown people can no longer accept responsibility for them. These punishments are solely owned by those who designed and implemented them.

There is a ray of hope as school districts across the country are starting to become "woke" to the idea that we can no longer exclude children of color from the learning community. School staff in major cities like NY and LA are now being trained in implicit bias, how to develop a culturally responsive educational lens, and the use of restorative practices with children. Scholars like Christopher Emdin (*For White Folks Who Teach in the Hood . . . and the Rest of Y'all Too*), Edward Furgus (*Solving Disproportionality and Achieving Equity*), and Gholdy Muhamad (*Cultivating Genius: An Equity Framework for Culturally and Historically Responsive Literacy*) are courageously leading the charge in how to effectively educate Black and Brown children. When he was in fifth grade, one of my sons threw a piece of paper across the room. I was called into the school and informed by the assistant principal that his teacher felt that my son created an unsafe environment for her and the rest of the students in the classroom. She requested a meeting with the administrator and her union representatives demanding that my son be suspended. The administrator indicated to me that while she understood that my son meant no harm to the teacher or his classmates, her hands were tied as the pressure from the teachers' union mounted. The teacher threatened to boycott the classroom until she had her "pound of flesh." My ten-year-old son had several adults—all of whom had more power than he did—working in concert against him. As a father, I was single minded in my purpose—to push against a system that had already labeled my son "dangerous." This was the same child that I held in my arms as a newborn. This was the same child that I roused from sleep each morning and herded into the shower. This was my son who was and is as handsome and charming as they come. His fifth-grade teacher had simply taken the baton from his first grade teacher, and she had a greater score to settle. Jantine Spilt and colleagues point out, "Teachers . . . foster emotional security and engagement in learning activities, which are necessary for adaptive school functioning and academic success [in children]." Conversely, strained relationships between teachers and their students were reported among "African American children with below-average literacy skills . . . [These students] are at risk of increasingly conflictual relationships with elementary school teachers from grade 1 to 5."[21] This information should shock all of us into doing better for our children. African American parents need to mobilize, to get the resources and knowledge to fight effectively for the rights of our children. School personnel should confront a history of disenfranchising students of color from the right to an education that prepares them to enter college and the twenty-first century workforce. Spilt correctly notes that this conflicted relationship between teachers and students has both a root cause and deleterious effect on our children. Such conflict may arise from:

- cultural misunderstanding and intergroup bias,
- low expectations of African American students,
- low quality relationships with the parents of African American students,
- cultural discontinuity between home and school, and
- absence of teachers from the cultures and communities of the children in the classroom.

Much of Split's argument can be summarized thusly: The educational system in the United States continues to be an agent of the racist policies that segregate schools. Students of color have never been given a fair chance— not in the classroom, not in the curriculum, and not in the suspension hearings. We have been stamped from the start. This is why our education system is in desperate need of what Benita Love calls an abolitionist approach to education.

Decolonizing the Curriculum

On January 19, 1998, the now disgraced Charlie Rose of PBS interviewed Toni Morrison about her work that focused on race. He reiterated the same question that Bill Moyour once asked her: "Can you imagine writing a novel that is not centered around race?" Her response was biting.

> Tolstoy writes about race all the time. So does Zola, so does James Joyce. Now if anybody can go up to an imaginary James Joyce and say you write about race all the time it's central in your novels. When are you going to write about—What? Because you see the person who asked about that question doesn't understand that he or she is also raced. So, to ask me when am I going to stop or if I can is to ask a question that in and of itself is its own answer. Yes I can write about white people, white people can write about Black people. Anything can happen in art. There are not boundaries there. Having to prove that I can do it is what was embarrassing or insulting.[22]

Rose, misunderstanding Morrison's point, pressed the issue. She responded:

> [It's] absurd to ask a Black writer to write about White people because a reputable journalist would not ask a prominent White writer, "When are you going to write about Black people?" Conversely, a writer who writes about the experiences of Black people consistently should not be questioned by the White journalist about writing about White people.[23]

This short exchange is prime example of White supremacy at work. Rose just could not understand that Morrison, with a CV that boasts a Pulitzer Prize, Nobel Prize, and the Presidential Medal of Freedom, didn't need to prove her literary legitimacy by writing about the lives of White people. She made the point that her writing about the Black experience was normed right alongside the works of Joyce, Dickinson, and other White writers. Again, that is part of the problem with dominant cultures. The White reader sees the stories of Black and Brown people as foreign and unusual, as other. Toni Morrison should never have to justify why she writes so much about the lives of Black folks. The same question is never asked of White writers.

I See Me in the Book

What do you picture when you hear the term "institutional racism"? Maybe you see a Black woman who's been passed over for a promotion everyone knew she deserved. Or, maybe you see a Black man being unjustly targeted by police. These are blatant examples of institutional racism, yes. But, there is a more insidious, silent racism plaguing our country that is just as, if not more, dangerous.

Gholdy Muhammad, in her book, *Cultivating Genius: An Equity Framework for Culturally and Historically Responsive Literacy*, notes, "When we frame the stories of people of color as narratives steeped in pain or even smallness, this becomes the dominant or sole representation."[24] Children of color need to see their faces, their languages, their music, their communities, and the genius of their ancestors represented in the books they read. How else will they know that their voices matter? That their stories matter? How else will they know that the world is willing to give space for their stories to be told? How else will they know that their ancestors survived so that their stories could be told in the lives of their descendants? Muhammad writes, "Rarely do young children learn about multiple figures in history who also contributed to excellence—in this case, those who can teach us ways to reframe our current education system." Dianne Johnson, in her article, "I See Me in the Book: Visual Literacy and African American Children's

Literature," maintains, "All young people, from all cultural backgrounds, need to see representations of themselves both visually and verbally."[25] These won't be visual or verbal representations, but ones that tell their stories authentically and in ways that are accessible and correlate to their lived experiences. Paulo Freire, in his groundbreaking work, *Pedagogy of the Oppressed,* maintains, "Education is suffering from narration sickness."[26]

Today, many school systems in the United States are trying to force fit culturally relevant materials into preexisting curricula. Teachers are trained to follow such curricula to fidelity and are discouraged from "free-range" teaching. Now, they are being told to look for supplementary materials to increase the lived experience of their students. How absurd. We can't demand that teachers make sweeping changes to their thinking, teaching approaches, or assessments without changing the curriculum. The lived experiences of Black and Brown people are not ancillary or supplemental. In a way, asking teachers to hunt for literature that represents Black and Brown students is degrading and disrespectful. Too long, curricula dominated by White stories and White storytellers have been at the center of urban education. It's time we courageously rewrite these curricula with Black and Brown people's experiences at the center. This would mean retelling the American Revolution and Civil Wars, the U.S. Constitution, and Lincoln's Emancipation Proclamation and the subsequent Reconstruction Period. Listen to most teachers teach these lessons and Blacks in particular and their voices have always sat on the margins, if at all. Curricula centered around the experiences, dignity, and heroism of my people would mean affirming the three-dimensional contributions of my ancestors. Rewriting the curricula would mean unmuting their voices. It would mean not whitewashing and even celebrating the genocidal atrocities perpetrated by the likes of Christopher Columbus and others. We may know the names of his three ships—barely necessary information for any generation—but do we know the names of the indigenous peoples that greeted those ships in peace but were met with war? Do we know the names of the dead tossed at sea during the slave trade? Do we know the names of those who survived? Do we know the names of the dead who fought in the Civil War and gave their lives in full measure without the promise of equality? Here, I am inspired by the words of Toni Morrison who argued that, as a writer of the Black experience, she stood at the border, at the margins and at the edge, claimed our story as central, and then invited the rest of the world to come to the place of the Black experience.

I See Me in the Teacher

I have been teaching two courses at Fordham University for the last ten years. I have always made a production out of the last day of class each semester. Students are encouraged to bring a favorite dish, a sort of multicultural pot-luck. While we eat, we reflect on the last fifteen weeks together. My students always look forward to our culminating session. As do I. Former students and neighboring professors are often drawn into the room by the tantalizing aromas of dishes from many cultures. It's an afternoon of good food, good conversation, and goodwill. In my opinion, it's the fondest of farewells.

Several years ago, on the last day of class, one student lingered behind after everyone cleaned up, broke down tables, secured the garbage, and filed out. She approached the lectern and, with tears in her eyes, thanked me for our work together during the semester. I accepted her gratitude but was puzzled by the intensity of emotion. "In all the years that I have been in college, I have never had a Black professor," she confessed. "Much less a Black professor with a PhD who is from my island—Jamaica." She said words couldn't express how good it felt to see me at the lectern teaching students of all ethnicities. She wiped the tears from her eyes and said, "Now I see that if you can do it, I think I can, too." This encounter was a humbling and sobering reminder that a curriculum is more than textbooks, syllabi, and assessments. As I left the building, I felt a deep sense of satisfaction for having drawn a roadmap for students of color of what is possible. At the center of the learning community must be the languages, cultures, lived experiences, and written curriculum that is representative of said community.

Not only do students of all ages need to see themselves in novels and history books, they need to have teachers that look like them. So many urban classrooms are staffed by White teachers who do not know how to relate to the students. Students of color need to see people that look and speak like their families standing in front of them as teachers, social workers, leaders. It goes without saying that such caring teachers and adults must be pedagogically and culturally competent. In fact, Gay as well as Milner both warn of "the danger in assuming that Black teachers, for instance, carry all the knowledge, skills, and commitments necessary to successfully teach African American students. To the contrary, there is a huge range of diversity even within groups, and we cannot oversimplify the characteristics of any group of teachers."[27]

More Male Teachers of Color Needed

Referencing the work of Brown, Nathaniel Bryan et al. note:

> Black teachers know how to engage in "purposeful teaching" to ensure the collective academic and social uplift of Black students. Purposeful teaching," they note, "is rooted in the notion that most Black teachers know the importance of building positive relationships with Black male and female students, centering race and community in teaching and learning, and helping Black students plan for the future.[28]

While many urban school districts have put forth a modicum of effort hiring and retaining male teachers of color, such efforts have yielded anemic results at best. Again, colleges and universities that are in the business of training the next generation of teachers must be intentional about recruiting, training, and supporting male students who are preparing to become educators. I won't bother to give you the depressing statistics of teachers who exit the classroom within the first five years of their teaching career. The authors further note, "Black male teachers possess the appropriate pedagogical performance style that can encourage Black male students to value their education and educational experience." These styles include the enforcer, the negotiator, and the playful. The enforcer helps the teacher maintain the expected standard in the classroom. The negotiator serves to resolve conflict and motivate students. The playful helps the teacher exchange jokes and ideas with Black male students as a way to break the monotony of the classroom. These are some of the nuanced textures within the African American culture that may be fumbled by a White teacher thereby increasing conflict, suspension rates, and the alienation of young Black men from the academic space.

Vereen and coauthors remind us that African American men often use humor and storytelling as a form of self-expression and communication. Such art forms are played out on Sunday morning in the pulpit and within the church pews. Attend any basketball game in our communities and you will hear biting humor and bantering on the basketball court. The same is true should you visit our barbershops on a Friday or Saturday night. Storytelling and humor travel with our young men of color into school buildings and into their classrooms as well. It is such storytelling and humor that so often gets young men of color swift and harsh disciplinary responses from teachers and school administrators. We have all heard school officials tell very different stories from young men of color about particular incidents in the classroom. Teachers use words like "disruption," "disrespectful," "dangerous," "unsafe," while Black and Brown boys use terms like, "joking with my friends," "cracking jokes on each other." Hearing these stories from young men often short circuits any meaningful conversation as school leaders chide them about the importance of "paying attention," "remaining on task," and the like. In the end, schools continuously miss the opportunity to honor the experiences of their students while teaching acceptable behaviors. "The art of storytelling has deep roots within the African American culture. For centuries, peoples of African descent have mastered and used this art to share thoughts and dreams, outline a context to explore history, and impart knowledge to the listener." In a classroom, storytelling is used allegorically and to model the trials and tribulations of daily life.[29]

Conclusion

Many fields of study (from anthropology to sociology to neurobiology) continue to remind us that one of the most important factors in a thriving human community is belonging. In its absence, children fail to learn all the academic and social skills needed to thrive in a 21st century world— not because they are incapable of learning and thriving, but because their learning community fails to love and nurture them into realizing their fullest human potential. Black male students in particular have received the least amount of love by the American school system. The evidence of this is quantified over and over again in school suspension rates across the country. The evidence of our failure to love them can be found in the dropout rate of boys of color, in their low graduation rate, in their absence from college campuses, and in their presence in the penitentiary system. When I speak of loving other people's children, I am not speaking of sentimentality or mushiness. I am speaking of liberating love. I am speaking of healing love. I am speaking of love that honors the experiences, stories, gifts, and talents of Black and Brown males in school systems across the United States. It's a kind of love that refuses to ignore the unique challenges that boys of color face daily in this country. This love courageously names systemic racism against boys of color as such. It pushes against educators and administrators that unjustly steer them towards special education programs. It brings the best pedagogy to the classroom every single day. It creates classroom environments of high expectations that constantly push young men of color to find their voices, to read texts that tell their stories. It's a love that can be found in classrooms that are as supportive as they are rigorous, caring as they are inclusive, and culturally responsive. This is the kind of love that Dr. Gholdy Muhammad speaks about when she argues that education should promote (a) identity, (b) skills, (c) intellect, (d) criticality, and (e) joy. This kind of love is desperately needed in education today.

Recently, I visited a school that experienced the tragic death of a student. My team and I were sent to support the school community during very tragic circumstances. We showed up on a Saturday as children streamed into the building to make sense of the senseless death of one of their beloved schoolmates. At some point, I stepped away from the incredible outpouring of grief to catch my breath and regulate my emotions. I walked into an empty classroom that had its own library. This was clearly a literature classroom. For the first time, I saw a rich library that had not only the classics, but books written by men and women that look like the children who were reading them. I saw the works of James Baldwin and Junot Diaz. I saw the works of Toni Morrison. I saw *The Bluest Eye, Beloved, Sula, Song of Solomon, Paradise, A Mercy, God Help the Child.* Some books were new and wanting wear and some old and torn from the fingers of children that searched the pages of those texts to bear witness to their own stories. Langston Hughes' collection of poems had a place in this compact library as did Maya Angelou and so many others. In the midst of the sorrow that I felt for this grieving community, I found peace in that empty room that was not so empty. I was surrounded by the pain, triumph, and wisdom of my ancestors. This classroom was filled with not only the teacher's love for literature that yelled, "representation matters," but with that teacher's love and respect for his or her students. When I speak of the moral imperative of learning to love other people's children, this is what I mean. When this love is fully present in a learning community, adults invest time, resources, and care in teaching prosocial behaviors. These behaviors can and should be taught alongside academics.

A loving educational community understands that it's counterintuitive to re-traumatize young Black men into compliance. Such a nurturing community no longer finds the need to remove and suspend kids for developmentally normal behaviors. This beloved community releases and replaces a punishment orientation with a restorative one. In my mind, this is what it means to love other people's children.

Notes

1. Christopher P. Chatmon and Jarvis R. Givens, eds., *We Dare Say Love: Supporting Achievement in the Educational Life of Black Boys* (Teachers College Press, 2019).
2. Dan Brooks, "Students Learn from People They Love," *New York Times* 17, no. 1 (2019).
3. Zaretta Hammond, *Culturally Responsive Teaching and the Brain: Promoting Authentic Engagement and Rigor among Culturally and Linguistically Diverse Students* (Corwin Press, 2014).

4. Ibram X. Kendi, *Stamped from the Beginning: The Definitive History of Racist Ideas in America* (Random House, 2017).

5. Sinthujaa Sampasivam, Katherine Anne Collins, Catherine Bielajew, and Richard Clément. "The Effects of Outgroup Threat and Opportunity to Derogate on Salivary Cortisol Levels," *International Journal of Environmental Research and Public Health* 13, no. 6 (2016): 616.

6. J. A. Everett, N. S. Faber, and M. Crockett, "Preferences and Beliefs in Ingroup Favoritism," *Frontiers in Behavioral Neuroscience* 9 (2015): 15.

7. Marcel Montrey and Thomas R. Shultz, "Outgroup Homogeneity Bias Causes Ingroup Favoritism," arXiv preprint, arXiv:1908.08203 (2019).

8. Bettina Love, "Dear White Teachers: You Can't Love Your Black Students If You Don't Know Them," *Education Week* 38, no. 26 (2019): 512–523.

9. W. Wright, "Fear of Black Students, Unfair Treatment Rampant in Denver Schools, Black Educators Say." Chalkbeat (2016).

10. Hani Morgan, "Misunderstood and Mistreated: Students of Color in Special Education," *Online Submission* 3, no. 2 (2020): 71–81.

11. Karen Prager, "Addressing Achievement Gaps: Positioning Young Black Boys for Educational Success," *Policy Notes* 19, no. 3 (Fall 2011).

12. Ibid.

13. NYC Department of Education, *Annual Special Education Data Report: School Year 2018–2019*, November 1, 2019. https://infohub.nyced.org/docs/default-source/default-document-library/annual-special-education-data-report-sy18-1960b79998ec27487584b9fedec3fac29c.pdf

14. Kimberly Young Wilkins, "Special Education Disability Classification 'Emotional Disturbance,'" memo to P-12 Education Committee, January 2, 2020, https://www.regents.nysed.gov/common/regents/files/120p12d1.pdf.

15. Moniqueka E. Gold, and Heraldo Richards. "To Label or Not to Label: The Special Education Question for African Americans," *Educational Foundations* 26 (2012): 143–156.

16. C. Anderson, *White Rage: The Unspoken Truth of Our Racial Divide* (Bloomsbury Publishing, 2016).

17. Carla R. Monroe, "African American Boys and the Discipline Gap: Balancing Educators' Uneven Hand." *Educational Horizons* 84, no. 2 (2006): 102–111.

18. A. Quereshi and J. Okonofua, "Locked Out of the Classroom: How Implicit Bias Contributes to Disparities in School Discipline," (2017).

19. Russell J. Skiba and Natasha T. Williams, "Are Black Kids Worse? Myths and Facts about Racial Differences in Behavior," *The Equity Project at Indiana University* (2014): 1–8.

20. Alicia Darensbourg, Erica Perez, and Jamilia J. Blake, "Overrepresentation of African American Males in Exclusionary Discipline: The Role of School-Based Mental Health Professionals in Dismantling the School to Prison Pipeline," *Journal of African American Males in Education* 1, no. 3 (2010).

21. Jantine L. Spilt and Jan N. Hughes, "African American Children at Risk of Increasingly Conflicted Teacher–Student Relationships in Elementary School," *School Psychology Review* 44, no. 3 (2015): 306–314.

22. Toni Morrison Beautifully Answers an "Illegitimate" Question on Race (Jan. 19, 1998) | Charlie Rose, YouTube

23. Ibid.
24. Gholdy Muhammad, *Cultivating Genius: An Equity Framework for Culturally and Historically Responsive Literacy i* (Scholastic Incorporated, 2020).
25. Dianne Johnson, "I See Me in the Book: Visual Literacy and African-American Children's Literature," *Children's Literature Association Quarterly* 15, no. 1 (1990): 10–13.
26. Paulo Freire, *Pedagogy of the Oppressed,* trans. Myra Bergman Ramos (New York, NY: Herder, 1972).
27. Iv Milner and H. Richard, "The Promise of Black Teachers' Success with Black Students," *Educational Foundations* 20 (2006): 89–104; G. Gay, G. (2000). Culturally, Responsive Teaching: Theory, Research, and Practice. (New York, NY: Teachers College Press, 2000); G. Gay, and K. Kirkland, "Developing Cultural Critical Consciousness and Self-Reflection in Preservice Teacher Education," *Theory into Practice* 42, no. 3 (2003): 181–187.
28. Nathaniel Bryan, Lamar Johnson, and Toni Milton Williams, "Preparing Black Male Teachers for the Gifted Classroom: Recommendations for Historically Black Colleges and Universities (Hbcus)." *The Journal of Negro Education* 85, no. 4 (2016): 489–504.
29. Linwood G. Vereen, Nicole R. Hill, and S. Kent Butler, "The Use of Humor and Storytelling with African American Men: Innovative Therapeutic Strategies for Success in Counseling," *International Journal for the Advancement of Counselling* 35, no. 1 (2013): 57–63.

6

Surrounded by a Great Cloud of Witnesses

Upon arriving in New York City in the Summer of 1992, my aunts took me to a small Pentecostal church at the base of a dilapidated apartment building at the intersection of North and South Broadway in Yonkers, just a short drive from the Bronx. It was in this small community that I found grace, faith, and an expanded life-long family. Here, I would begin a new journey with the Divine, one filled with love and acceptance, fellowship and community, a journey of knowledge and empowerment.

The Church of God of Prophecy is an international faith community with churches throughout the world. My grandparents served faithfully in the Church of God of Prophecy in Jamaica. We continued that tradition here in the United States. By the time I stood on the steps of the little church in Yonkers, my aunties, uncles, and many of my cousins who had migrated a few years earlier from Jamaica were well integrated into the congregation. That Summer in 1992, I was welcomed with open arms. Thirty years later, I look back with a deep sense of gratitude and appreciation for

No Country For Black Men, pages 89–112
Copyright © 2023 by Information Age Publishing
www.infoagepub.com
89

the love, acceptance, and firm foundation that this church gave me when I first set foot on American soil.

It was the first time in my life that I felt a part of something bigger than myself and my family. These people were strangers, yet they welcomed and accepted me without reservation or condition. I was one with these people. They helped me to find my voice in this daunting and strange land— through playing, praying, singing, preaching, volunteering, dialogue, and fellowship. I found my emerging adult identity in this church. It was also here that I would eventually find the woman of my dreams. This experience reminds me again and again of the importance of community.

As a child, I spent most of my time in my head. Sitting alone with my thoughts was easy for me. Wandering in the Jamaican woods by myself was natural. It was not at all difficult remaining apart from my peers. I simply preferred my own company. No one questions you when you're alone. There are no arguments, no awkward moments, no misunderstandings. As comfortable and safe as that solitude was, there was also little incentive to grow. I didn't enjoy the same seclusion in my new faith community.

It was impossible to live among these people and remain apart. My pastor often spoke with me about my faith and the future. He exposed me to basic literature like reading the newspaper, Time Magazine, the scriptures, and non-literature like my social environment. Older church members went to youth meetings to support us and to show interest in our well-being. This was an amazing experience for me. In this new and brave space that was co-constructed by leaders and laity, I was not able to retreat into the safety of solitude. These people pulled me out of my shell through weekly activities and intergenerational interactions. It was exactly what this 17-year-old immigrant needed. Within a year, I was leading the youth group, teaching Sunday school classes, and preaching regularly. Over time, my confidence and competence grew.

There was a stark dichotomy between the community that I found in this small American church and what I experienced in my American high school. In school, I was just one among a sea of faceless teens. In church, my "somebodiness" was validated and celebrated. When we gathered on Sundays, we greeted each other with authentic smiles and ended with fellowship. We addressed each other as "brother" and "sister," and that's what we were to each other—family.

I often look back at this time in my life and wonder why there aren't more conversations about how these kinds of experiences can nurture and mold us into successful leaders and citizens of the world. In *Soul Mates: Religion, Sex, Love and Marriage Among African Americans and Latinos,* sociologists

W. Bradford Wilcox and Nicholas Wolfinger show that when situated in community, we are "more likely to be working, avoid crime and incarceration, and get married."[1] In other words, connection to faith and faith communities can serve as major protective factors for men of color. This is also supported by research done by Pew Institute which indicates that the Black church does indeed help with issues of equity. This includes employment opportunities and sermons that address political hot buttons. The survey revealed that a high percentage of participants indicated that it is

> essential that houses of worship offer spiritual comfort (72 percent), a sense of community and fellowship (71 percent), moral guidance (66 percent), assistance to the needy with bills, housing and food (55 percent), practical job and life skills (44 percent) and a sense of racial affirmation or pride (43 percent).[2]

We are at our best when we find community. It is in community that we grow, develop, learn empathy, sacrifice, and the power of collective vision-advocacy. And, at last, it is in community that we learn to mourn when death comes. We also learn to offer comfort and healing to the broken heart and restoration and forgiveness to those who breach the moral codes and practices of the community. I saw all of this in my community of faith. It is why I have spent much of my career advocating for creating healthy communities in the workplace, school house, church house, and first and foremost, in the family system.

Through My Father's Eyes: Lessons From My Paternal Home

I remember visiting my father in Kingston, Jamaica a few days before I left for NY. He was working at a morgue. I wanted to sit with him and tell him that I would be leaving Jamaica permanently. I wanted to tell him that the future would be better for all of us because of this opportunity. None of those words came out of my mouth. "I am not sure when I will see you again," I told him. He might have said something like, "I am happy for you." The silence that descended was thick with all the words I wanted to say, with all the words he said with his eyes. "There's something I want to show you," he said after a time. I followed him to the back where the dead were kept in refrigerators. As a child, I was terrified of being anywhere near the dead. The few funerals I went to had haunted me for months after. As we approached a large door, my anxiety became a palpable thing. My heart beat a sharp staccato in time with our footfalls. I felt sweat gathering on my brow. My breaths came in short, muted gasps. I did *not* want to see what was behind that door. My father, unaware of my terror, threw wide the gate to my nightmare. And, that's when I learned that life can be so much more tragic than anything I could imagine.

Lying inert in a refrigerated compartment was the body of a young man whose life had been cut short because of the choices that he made, because of the gang that he ran with, because of the community violence all too common in his world.

My father wanted to show me what he could not tell me. I didn't need the words. I got his message loud and clear. "When you get to America, be careful. Do the right thing. Stay out of trouble." My father's heart has since stopped beating. He now rests with the ancestors.

Thirty years later and now having two sons of my own, I am more appreciative of my late father's valiant attempt to save me from gang violence, risk taking behaviors, the penitentiary—the cold and unforgiving refrigerator. Over the years I have allowed myself to drift back to that conversation. It is the only conversation with my father that is crystalized in my memory. It is the only one that has not faded with the washing of time. And yet, more than my father's last-ditch effort to impart some fatherly advice, it was really this small church community that saved me.

The church, and particularly the Black church, has been described as:

> The Black controlled independent denominations, which make up the heart of Black Christians and is principally concerned with the expressions of spirituality and the religious practices of African Americans. It also serves as the functional family for its congregants and community and serves a plethora of vital social and economic functions. It continues to be the primary location of Black political activity and the vehicle through which Blacks can address the dominant social order and relate to their God through their cultural heritage.[3]

Away from the dominant gaze, away from spaces where we do not always feel welcome, away from spaces where we are often treated as less, we gather together wearing our Sunday best. At church, women and men get to wear outfits that would not be accepted in the marketplace. Decked out in our "Sunday best," we exude pride, confidence, art, elegance, and beauty, traits that are often not welcomed or recognized elsewhere. Away from the dominant gaze we greet each other with "holy hugs and kisses" without fear of rejection. Away from the dominant gaze, we sing songs that speak of our liberation from our oppressors. We dance until we are soaked in sweat. We form choirs, choruses, praise and worship teams, step teams, and drama teams. We dance to music so loud that it would drive many mad. This was what I found in my faith community all those years ago. Here, my Blackness did not offend God. It was not a threat to His love. Here, I was the future of the church. I was a terrible singer, but they nevertheless gave me a mic. I was a nervous wreck when I spoke, and yet they gave me the opportunity to hone my oratory skills.

Today, as a seasoned preacher and lecturer, I see this same trajectory in the lives of many young men and women in my faith community. In his book, *Community: The Structure of Belonging*, Peter Block reminds us that despite all the advances in technology, we are still very much disconnected from each other. He notes, "All this does not create the connection from which we can become grounded and experience the sense of safety that arises from a place where we are emotionally, spiritually, and psychologically a member."[4] Again, we all need belonging. I found belonging, membership, and my voice in this small but ever-expanding community.

In his insightful article, "Supporting Black Churches: Faith, Outreach, and the Inner-City Poor," John Dilulio Jr. notes, "Young men from poverty-stricken neighborhoods who attend church on a regular basis exponentially increase their chances of subverting a life of poverty, crime and other social ills."[5] I might have been that young man who became a son and brother to strangers. Fortunately, because my faith community stepped in and supported me, that didn't happen. Human behavioralists Robert Joseph Taylor and Linda M. Chatters make some important points about how members of local churches support each other. "Pastoral care is the overarching construct which incorporates and expresses the supportive features of the church."[6] Such support can be understood not only in material terms but also as creating spaces of belonging through social and emotional support. Even public education systems are taking a "pastoral care" approach to supporting students and their families.

As a pastor, I am used to ministering to the sick, the elderly, the poor and marginalized. Thus, it wasn't a stretch to bring this same theory of care to my work as a public-school administrator. I saw how some staff struggled with the idea of leaving the school building to visit families in their homes. Some felt that this was outside of their job description, while others were apprehensive about unknown, potentially dangerous variables such as negotiating dimly lit stairwells and countless other "what ifs." Outliers notwithstanding, I have always found allies who support meeting families where they live. This was the pastoral care that I received growing up in a small faith community. The elderly members of the community were not forgotten. The young were not ignored. I saw this rich and responsive approach to support that was new to me outside of my family. Growing up in a large intergenerational family, we children were regularly tasked with transporting Sunday lunch to elderly family members. We were tasked with reporting to those homes to gather firewood for cooking. We went food shopping. Now, these values were expanded to nonfamily members.

I soaked it up. I sat in homes and listened to stories. I broke bread with families at their dinner tables. We read scriptures to the sick. We prayed for those who lost loved ones. We collected funds to help with burial expenses. I saw counseling in full action by people who never stepped foot into a graduate counseling class. Admittedly, I learned much of my clinical and advocacy skills not from textbooks or my university instructors, but from the elders of my church. Those moments of being present with the disen-franchised, doing group work with youth and community members were invaluable. They helped to mold me into a more competent, compassion-ate human being. To this point, Taylor and Chatters add:

- Black churches have been responsive to the needs of the com-munity whose access to traditional social institutions has been restricted.
- Unlike many other institutions, Black churches are completely financed, built, and controlled by Blacks.
- The multifaceted roles and functions of churches in Black com-munities make them one of the most important social institutions second only to the family unit.
- Black churches are heavily involved in meeting the material, emotional, and spiritual needs of the community.
- It is the highest form of self-appraisal. You belong here. You have been placed here by the Divine. You cannot be anything less than what God has created you to be.[7]

This has been the scope of some of the support that I received in my faith community. In fact, that same church on the border of North and South Broadway would be the very place where I met my wife. I met and fell in love at eighteen with my pastor's daughter, Senikha Reece. It is because of this church that I have friends all across the globe—from Africa to South and Central America, from the Caribbean and Canada to the rest of North America, Asia, and Europe.

We Must Do More to Support Black Men

Historically, the Black church has not only provided a safe haven for Black men, it has also been one of America's better angels, confronting racism head on and working for justice for Black Americans. In fact, the Black church as an independent body "emerged as a protest against the racist theology and the racist ecclesiology of the church in America."[8] The enslavement of Black men and their families was legitimized as the very will of God. Such claims were also backed up with a "literal" interpretation of scripture that apparently supported the enslavement of others.[9] In many White communities today, God is still upheld as an ally of White supremacy. Jesus is White; angels are White; heaven is White. The devil is Black; sin is Black; hell is Black. You get the idea.

From the start, the Black church had to strike a distinction between a God who sides with White men and oppresses Black men and Black men whose mission it is to solicit a relationship with a God who sides with the oppressed. A rich body of experience of oppression, African culture, and exodus scriptures provided the raw material for a theology of liberation and celebration.

James H. Cone, also known as the father of liberation theology, linked the treatment of African Americans in the United States with the treatment of Jesus in ancient Palestine.

> The lynching tree joined the cross as the most emotionally charged symbols of the African American community—symbols that represented both death and the promise of redemption, judgment and the offer of mercy, suffering and the power of hope. Both the cross and the lynching tree represented the worst in human beings and at the same time an unquenchable ontological thirst for life that refuses to let the worst determine our final meaning.

In other words, Jesus was treated like a Black man—abused, unjustly jailed, brutalized by police, tried and convicted in a system guaranteed to convict him, and lynched on the cross. And, like Jesus, the killing of Black men by law enforcement was not hidden. It was sanctioned. Cone notes that lynching "could not have happened without widespread knowledge and the explicit sanction of local and state authorities and with tacit approval from the federal government, members of the white media, churches, and universities."[10] The entire societal apparatus conspired and congealed against Black men with deathly efficiency. At the center of this liberation proclamation are Black men (and, of course, Black women). Harvard scholar and literary critic, Henry Louis Gates, writes:

> Without the role of the Black Church, the Civil Rights Act of 1964, and the Voting Rights Act of 1965—signed into law by President Lyndon Johnson, without King by his side at both, and future congressman John Lewis, himself an ordained Baptist minister, present in 1965—would never have been enacted when they were. There is no question that the Black Church is a

parent of the civil rights movement, and today's Black Lives Matter movement is one of its heirs.[11]

One of the threats facing Black churches today is the migration to White conservatism that is blind, deaf, and dumb to the persistent suffering of Blacks within their church communities. Yet, it was the church that organized marches and sit-ins. It was Black men, women, and children who faced down biting dogs and the hose in the deep south. Cone was right when he said, "It was the 'African' side of Black religion that helped African-Americans to see beyond the white distortions of the gospel and to discover its true meaning as God's liberation of the oppressed from bondage."[12] Today, many scholars argue that the Black Church has drifted so far away from its core mission of liberation that it would not even know how to find its way back even if it tried.

The Regression of the Black Church

The Black church of today bears little resemblance to the Black church of the past. It has moved away from evangelizing a social gospel to focus on a more hyper-spiritual and personal faith experience. Because of this, it is seen as "passive," "other-worldly," and not inclined to struggle for racial, economic, social, or political justice.[13] Today the gospel that is preached to the poor has been replaced with the prosperity gospel. If the gospel to the poor is one of hope and advocacy, the prosperity gospel is about the individual doing whatever it takes to become wealthy. It's about self and self-indulgence. "The Black Church," Eddie Glaude argues, "is alienated from the moment in which it lives."[14] Consequently, we have become co-opted by the moment. In a very real sense, our prophetic fire has been extinguished. We don't fight for liberation, for justice, for righteousness. Instead, we occupy our time with messages and causes that are nonessential. Our church services and liturgies, while entertaining, lack a spirit that transforms.[15]

If that is not enough:

- Unemployment is at its highest in 25 years (as of 2010).
- Thirty-five percent of our children live in poverty.
- Inadequate healthcare, rampant incarceration, home foreclosures, and a general sense of helplessness overwhelm many of our brethren.[16]

We have taken up causes such as protesting against same sex unions, climate change, and the appointment of liberal justices to the U.S. Supreme Court.

Some forty years before Glaude penned his scathing article, "The Black Church Is Dead," Calvin Marshall raised serious questions about the role the church must play in the struggle for the total liberation of Black people. "Unfortunately, as the church entered the 20th century...other priorities seemed to replace the burning zeal that the church once displayed for liberation."[17] We have turned our backs on our history and legacy, forgetting the works of Frederick Douglas, Martin Luther King, Charles Price, James W. Hood and Alexander B. Walters, Mordecaai Johnson, Benjamin Mays, George Kelsey Adam Clayton Powell Jr, Andrew Young, and Joseph Lowery, among others, who gave their lives, time and fire to the liberation of African Americans.[18] Marshall notes:

> Trips to the Holy Land become more important than trips through the streets of her impoverished neighborhoods—to see, to feel, to hear, and to taste, the plight of her people. She became an organization of joiners, she built her structures, organized her self-indulgent programs and then opened her doors and invited good, orderly and decent people to come. She forgot her mission was one of salvation–liberation and she ceased to be found in the arenas where men were struggling to throw off the yoke of oppression and slavery. She no longer understood her role in terms of revolution and change. She became status quo oriented and stagnant. In doing so, she not only betrayed her founding fathers, she also betrayed the Christ whose gospel she yet claimed to be preaching.

Black preachers attempting to model their message and ministry after Kenneth Copeland, Rick Warren, or Joel Osteen will not do. It won't do because, every day, the very existence of our sons and daughters hangs in the balance. What is noteworthy about the current direction of the Black Church is that we have left the rich and fierce fire of advocacy for something anemic and toothless. What many churches are attracted to today is a feel good, individualized, prosperity gospel that moves seamlessly and interchangeably between the White and Black pulpits. When we step away from those pulpits, we soon realize that these messages will never be congruent with the suffering of the people in our communities. It is shameful to see how we have lost our heritage of advocating for the disenfranchised, marginalized, and ostracized. Cone notes, "If we intended to fight on a theological and intellectual level as a way of empowering our historical and political struggle for justice, we had to create a new theological movement, one that was derived from and thus accountable to our people's fight for justice."[19] That fight resulted in the Civil Rights Act of 1964 and the Voting Rights Act of 1965. That fight has lost its steam in some ways today. Still, the evidence does show that Black churches continue their traditions.

In 1992, Mark Chaves and Lynn Higgins compared the kinds of community engagement that Black and White churches were engaged in. Their research revealed, "Black congregations were significantly more likely to participate in meal services, civil rights activities, community development initiatives and public education on disease." This should not surprise any of us. If we are to live out the social gospel that Jesus advanced—caring for the least, the last, and the lost—then our work must be in solidarity with the work of Christ. What's more, the Black church has an obligation to not only name the root cause of such suffering but respond to it in concrete ways. White churches, on the other hand, are "significantly more likely to participate in recreational programs for youth, right-to-life actions and refugee-related programs."[20] The subversive danger here for Black churches, especially those that are tied to White central leadership, is that the call and mission of the church becomes subsumed with activities that are not responsive to the blistering needs of the communities we serve.

This same dilemma exists in multiracial congregations. In the words of Dr. King, in the United States, Sunday morning is the most segregated hour. Well, then, let's create more diverse churches, right? Unfortunately, this solution does not work in today's America. In fact, as Chaves and Higgins note, the mission of White and Black churches are often vastly different in how they carry out the gospel. Further studies are needed to evaluate multiracial, Black, and White churches' response to the social, economic, and political issues facing this nation. In their book, *Divided by Faith*, Michael Emerson and Christian Smith note that evangelicals, and White evangelicals in particular, "likely do more to perpetuate the racial divide than to tear it down"[21] because they often fail to name the deleterious impact of White supremacy on the Black and Brown community.

So, while you might see multiracial worshipers streaming into mega churches on Sunday mornings, you must ask yourself:

- How do those congregations respond to the pressing social and economic issues of our time?
- How are those sermons addressing bigotry and discrimination not just in society but within those congregations?
- What spaces are created to have honest discussions about racism in society?

The working assumption that people worshiping together must mean that all racial divides have been bridged is a faulty one. (Granted, such gatherings can be designed to address the protracted racial animus in this country.) Instead, we should seek answers to the following: "How do multiracial congregations stifle cultural expressions in our worship, music, sermonic forms, fellowship, and community support and activism?" These are fundamental questions that must be addressed before we green light multiracial congregations as the answer to racism in our churches. There is no point to having such worship services when congregants leave church to return to their separate zip codes and their separate socioeconomic statuses. We need more than gatherings. We need a more just world for all God's children. Multiracial churches should leverage the gospel by preaching what Mark Roelofs calls:

1. *Radical* Egalitarianism—White America must divest itself of the notion that it is superior. On the other hand, our churches should use the opportunity to leverage Christian principals. Such endeavors must lead to affirming the fact that "all human beings are, existentially, equal. The distinctions between them drawn in our social orders—by age, sex, wealth, power, skills, learning, beauty and so on—are all of little, artificial and passing significance."[22] This, Roelofs argues, is rooted in the words of the Apostle Paul: "There is neither Jew nor Greek, there is neither male nor female; for you are all one in Christ Jesus" (Galatians 3:28). Though taken out of context, this very passage has been co-opted by colorblind racism.
2. *Radical Communitarianism*—This communitarianism challenges the White church and, by extension, White America to reflect, repent, and confront the structural and institutional racialized society that it has built and maintained over hundreds of years. In a way, this self-confrontation would be an existential crisis of letting go of the notion that one is better than another on the basis of some socially constructed reality. This confrontation becomes an identity crisis: that White is not better than Black, blue eyes are not better than brown, White children are no more deserving of a good education than Black children. This radical communitarianism was demonstrated by Christ when he gave his life for all people, by loving all people. Boasting that people of all colors show up for worship on Sunday morning is not enough. It is merely a start.

A Call to Reconversion of the Black Church

One of my favorite authors is Protestant theologian, Walter Brueggemann. In his now classic, *The Prophetic Imagination,* Brueggemann not only names the problem with the church but, using a rich body of scripture, proposes a way to subvert its pervasive numbness to the suffering of the world. He opens with these words, "The contemporary American church is so largely enculturated to the American ethos of consumerism that it has little power to believe or act."[23] This, unfortunately, is true for most denominations today. This enculturation, according to Brueggemann, is a direct consequence of the "abandonment of faith tradition." This is certainly true for the Black church. Brueggemann argues that the only way for the church to find its power to act and to believe is to return to its tradition. In this case, the Black church must return to its roots and mission of ministering to the whole person. It must engage in radical advocacy rather than being "co-opted and domesticated" by the dominant culture. The truth of the matter is that we have all been influenced by colonialism and White supremacy. As such, our work as a people and as a church must be to unlearn what we were taught about ourselves as a people, the world as constructed by White supremacy, and the god of that world while fighting to dismantle the impact of such construction.

In *Decolonizing Preaching: The Pulpit as Postcolonial Space,* Sarah Travis reminds us: "The ethos of the empire is so ingrained in modern consciousness there is barely room to consider alternative systems."[24] For the Black preacher, this begins with ensuring that the stories we tell in our preaching are never told through the dominant narrative that further oppresses people of color. In our sermonic discourses, we must side with the oppressed and oppose the oppressor both in scripture and in the world. We must develop a hermeneutic of suspicion, notes Travis. Furthermore, we must never be naive about the role White evangelicalism plays in perpetuating racism in Christianity and in the world of politics.

In *White Evangelical Racism: The Politics of Morality in America*, Anthea Butler notes, "Racism is a feature, not a bug of American evangelicalism."[25] Again, I return to the notion that multiracial worship services are dominated by White supremacy. It was White evangelicalism that gave us Donald Trump. Christian conservatives donated handily to his campaign. They prayed for him. They promoted him as a messenger of God. They went out and voted for him. And, when he lost the second time, they stormed the capital on January 6, 2021 using the fallacy that the election was stolen as justification. Butler also reminds us of the words of one of the nation's most celebrated evangelical heroes, Billy Graham, who, when asked to comment on Dr. King's "I Have a Dream" speech, said, "Only when Christ comes again will little white children of Alabama walk hand in hand with little Black children."

I like what Randy Woodley said in his interview with Bo Sanders on Decolonizing Evangelicalism:

Jesus said, love your enemies. I don't think Jesus simply meant for us not to hate our enemies. That seems to be where most evangelicals are comfortable leaving things: Just don't be a hater. But, the opposite of love is not in fact hate. Hatred implies an emotional investment, meaning that we actually care about the people we hate, right? Hate has to be maintained and is often driven by passion. We just hate to admit we have emotional investment in those we claim to hate. No, the opposite of love is not hate. The binary opposite of love is apparent in such attitudes as indifference, superficiality, disconnectedness, presumed superiority and individualism.[26]

It is this indifference that inspires numbness and inaction on the part of both the Black and White churches. It seems that we are satisfied with condolences and a prayer when White supremacy creeps into our dreams and leaves nightmares behind.

On June 17, 2015, Dylann Roof walked casually into the Emanuel African Methodist Episcopal Church also known as "Mother Emanuel," sat in Bible study and then, at some point, pulled out a gun and fired upon the members of that church killing nine people including its senior pastor and state senator Clementa C. Pinckney. In one of his jailhouse confessions Roof said, "I would like to make it crystal clear; I do not regret what I did. I am not sorry. I have not shed a tear for the innocent people I killed."[27] These were the words of a stone-cold killer whose mind was poisoned against Black people. While the South Carolina church community was reeling from this heinous crime against their beloved pastor and church members at the hand of White supremacy, the rest of the country was again offering condolences and a prayer. Christian Smith writes, "The massacre elicited much religious language in public commentary, including claims that the redemptive power of God was needed to help the community heal and overcome racism, that Dylann Roof would be judged by God for his acts, that he would burn in hell, and that no evil could overcome the saving love of Jesus Christ. Smith continues, "the most relevant commentary following the murders was the common claim that the killer, Dylann Roof, was not simply acting as a violent racist bigot, but was an agent of Satan, of the devil the superhuman personification of evil who stands in absolute opposition to God."[28] Unfortunately, this is the common default language that is often used after White supremacy is turned loose on communities of color. First, our White counterparts scold us for talking about the need for gun control in light of these mass shootings. Guns don't kill people, people kill people. Secondly, prayer and condolences are offered as a final offering as though that is enough. Thirdly, the blame is taken out of the hand of the killer and the system that poisoned his mind against Black and Brown bodies. This is the work of Satan we are told—the devil made me do it. Finally, we engage in a larger conversation about mental health. Far too many people know that Dylann Roof needed access to mental health care and didn't get it. We dance around the root cause—White supremacy, which sent Dylann Roof to sit in a Bible study session in the basement of Mother Emanuel AME church and then turn a gun on them. We must do more than offer prayers, condolences, and blame Satan for the unjust structures of society that continue to claim the lives of Black and Brown bodies. And yes, we must do more to strengthen mental health support for all those that need it, as I noted in Chapter 4. In the words of the Rev. Lenny Duncan, Jesus is Trayvon Martin, armed only with a bag of Skittles and an iced tea against an entire world that would rather hang him from a tree than love him. Until we see this, we are lost."[29]

Pastoral Circle: Reclaiming Our Prophetic Fire

In his autobiography, Frederick Douglas had this to say about Christianity:

> What I have said respecting and against religion, I mean strictly to apply to the slave-holding religion of this land and with no possible reference to Christianity proper; for, between the Christianity of this land, and the Christianity of Christ, I recognize the widest possible difference—so wide, that to receive the one as good, pure, and holy, is of necessity to reject the other as bad corrupt and wicked... To be the friend of the one, is of necessity to be the enemy of the other. I love the pure, peaceable, and impartial Christianity of Christ: I therefore hate the corrupt, slaveholding, women-whipping, cradle-plundering, partial and hypocritical Christianity of this land.[30]

Douglas was exasperated by the duality and hypocrisy of the Christianity of his time and challenged the church to find congruence between their practices and the Christ that they proclaimed. In a way, we are at that crossroads today with our hyper-spiritual and prosperity gospel that seems so distant from the message of the Cross. We have lost our prophetic fire because we have removed ourselves from the places where Black men and their families live, work, and suffer. In some cases, our eyes see without bearing witness, our ears hear without evoking an ounce of empathy or righteous indignation. To respond to our pervasive numbness, I would like to propose a pastoral circle as a possible methodological approach to becoming more alive to the suffering of Black men and boys in our community.

Pastoral circle, also known as the "circle of praxis" or "hermeneutic circle," was developed within the Jesuit tradition in the 1970s and 1980s and popularized in the work of Joe Holland and Peter Henriot in their book, *Social Analysis: Linking Faith and Justice*.[31] The framework proposes four primary moves when responding to issues of justice. They are, (a) insertion, (b) social analysis, (c) theological reflection, and (d) pastoral planning or action. The model is derived from the concept of seeing, judging, and acting in the name of justice. For the purposes of this body of work, I would like to employ the pastoral circle framework narrowly to address how the church and specifically the Black church can reclaim its prophetic fire in supporting Black men.

Putting Ourselves on the Scenes of Suffering

One of the challenges that Black church leaders face today is that many of us do not live in the communities where our houses of worship are located. We swoop in a few times a week, hold services and meetings, and then retreat back into our cloistered world. We are removed from the struggles of the people we are supposed to serve. We lack the texture of the community. This is a common complaint about White police officers that serve our communities of color, White teachers that teach in urban schools, but rarely one about our church leaders who only frequent church communities for services and meetings. We drive past the homeless, the shuttered businesses, the dilapidated houses untroubled and unmoved to respond. We accept police arresting young Black men as a part of the landscape of urban life. Pastoral circle invites us to insert ourselves into the spaces and lived experiences of Black men.

Bryan Stevenson, an attorney and fierce advocate of the incarcerated, advances the profound concept of the power of proximity. He argues, "Proximity to the condemned and incarcerated made the question of each person's humanity more urgent and meaningful, including my own." He continues, "Proximity has taught me some basic and humbling truths, including this vital lesson: Each of us is more than the worst thing we've ever done. My work with the poor and the incarcerated has persuaded me that the opposite of poverty is not wealth, the opposite of poverty is justice."[32] The Black church must find ways to advocate, educate and, yes, celebrate the strengths of Black men if it is to combat their sustained oppression in the United States—for well over 400 years. Jesus and, by extension, the Christianity that Frederick Douglas spoke about, demands that we become the Good Samaritan who is unafraid to stop, nurse bleeding wounds, and find places of healing for our brothers who suffer unjustly. We must put ourselves on the scene where humans suffer.

Social Analysis—Prophetic Interpretation of Society's Data

Social analysis is critical because it demands that we become astute to the social, economic, historical, and political forces at play in maintaining the sustained oppression of Black men at all levels of society. It requires that we answer the question, "Why is this happening?"

- Why do 50 percent of young men of color never graduate from high school?[33]
- Why is it that African American men have a one in four chance of being incarcerated?[34]
- Why is it that between "1950 and 2010 the average combined death rate for Black males aged fifteen to twenty-four who died in the United States due to homicide and suicide was 93.5 per 100,000"?[35]
- Why is it that "in 2019, the rate for Black men (participating in the labor force) was 64.8 percent, which was 4.4 percentage points lower than the rate of 69.2 percent for men overall."?[36]
- Why is it that the mortality rate of Black men is more dismal than any other ethnic group historically and presently?[37]

Churches must be able to read the signs of the times, interpret data, explore root causes, and work to address those issues through advocacy and activism. Suffice it to say that no one church might be able to address every social, educational, economic, or political issue, but we all must do something to support those living on the margins. Protestant and denominational church leaders must move away from over-spiritualizing the brokenness of this world by simply lamenting it as the work of Satan and leaving it at that. We must become pastor-sociologists, pastor-anthropologists, and pastor-activists who study and resist the historical and current forces at work against men of color. In *The Black Messiah*, Reverend Albert Cleage Jr. writes about this kind of militaristic, prophetic fire: "Black Americans need to know that the historical Jesus was a leader who went about among the people of Israel, seeking to root out the individualism and identification with their oppressor which had corrupted them, and to give them faith in their own power to rebuild the nation."[38] This analysis is not only a cursory glance at the data, it is naming root causes of the data using a prophetic lens that exposes what the reigning White supremacy wants to hide. And, all those Black preachers who continue to call themselves prophets but do not proclaim justice, do not advocate for those existing on the margins should be challenged into "seeing, judging, and acting."

Theological Reflection—What Would Jesus Do With the Data?

Theological reflection allows us to examine what our faith traditions as well as scriptures have to say about social issues. Dietrich Bonhoeffer, in his classic book on cultivating authentic Christian community, notes, "A Christian fellowship lives and exists by the intercession of its members for one another, or it lapses."[39] This intercession must move beyond prayer to action. Prayers offered for the victimized that are not followed by action are impotent. People of color were the victims of a mass shooting as recently as May 2022 in Buffalo, New York when a White supremacist drove two hours to shoot up a supermarket in the name of hate. Prayers are sent up for the many Black bodies that are incarcerated, unemployed, diseased, demonized but very little action accompanies those fervent prayers. The apostle James was right. "Faith without works is dead" (James 2:26). Theological reflection invites us to use scriptures as a primary body of evidence to act against injustice and on behalf of the marginalized. It's the story of Esther and Mordecai advocating for a people that were under existential threat from the ruling group. It was Abraham who advocated for the citizens of Sodom and Gomorrah. It was Jesus who advocated for the children, the widows, the differently abled persons, the poor, foreigners, and those under the rule of the Roman Empire. Theological reflection involves activating the sacred text to support the work that we must do ourselves. Jesus did his part in the perpetual fight for justice, and so must we. Billy Graham had it wrong when he said we had to wait for the return of Jesus to see the light of justice shining down on us. We must become coworkers with Christ in advancing justice for all in our time.

Sandra Barnes notes, "Black Church members have been shown to develop symbols such as rituals, songs, sayings, sacred meetings and biblical stories to help them interpret events, focus efforts and provide organizational vision."[40] The idiom from the late 1980s and early 1990s would hold true here: "What would Jesus do?" But, it's not just about scriptural response. Such reflection also invites us to consider movements, prophets, and pioneers of more recent times that worked relentlessly to turn the wheels of justice. Dr. King, Malcolm X, Frederick Douglass, and others courageously gave their last measure to affirm our basic rights to life, liberty, and the pursuit of happiness.

An example of theological reflection might be reading the Good Samaritan story with a fresh lens. The traditional interpretation focuses on the man that is robbed, beaten, and left half dead. The priest and Levite pass without responding. Enter the Good Samaritan, the unexpected hero in the story. But, what if more attention is paid to the robbers? For 400 years, African American men have been robbed of our dignity, beaten, rejected by society, and labeled dangerous. We languish between life and death, literally and figuratively. Theological reflection must invite us to:

- Address crime infested Jericho Road and those that prey on the innocent.
- Hold the Levite and the priest accountable for abandoning their fellow traveler because they have become numb to the suffering of others. These are the White and Black clergy leaders of our time that are too busy to stop and deal with the problem of injustice. In his letter from Birmingham Jail, MLK had this to say about his fellow Christians who became numb to the plight of African American fight for justice:

> I must make two honest confessions to you, my Christian and Jewish brothers. First, I must confess that over the past few years I have been gravely disappointed with the white moderate. I have almost reached the regrettable conclusion that the Negro's great stumbling block in his stride toward freedom is not the White Citizen's Councilor or the Ku Klux Klanner, but the White moderate, who is more devoted to "order" than to justice; who prefers a negative peace which is the absence of tension to a positive peace which is the presence of justice; who constantly says: "I agree with you in the goal you seek, but I cannot agree with your methods of direct action"; who paternalistically believes he can set the timetable for another man's freedom; who lives by a mythical concept of time and who constantly advises the Negro to wait for a "more convenient season." Shallow understanding from people of good will is more frustrating than absolute misunderstanding from people of ill will. Lukewarm acceptance is much more bewildering than outright rejection.[41]

It's incredible how we so often focus on the KKK or, more recently, The Proud Boys and Oath Keepers as our primary threats to racial justice. However, the more insidious and dangerous groups are those who shake hands with us in the workplace and in houses of worship, the teachers who eject kids from class and evict them from school, the police officers who engage in stop and frisk, the judge who distributes harsh sentences for minor infractions, the college admissions requirements that let some in and lock others out. We should be worried about Donald Trump who met with a bipartisan group of senators at the White House and referred to Haiti and African nations as "shithole countries."[42] The priest and the Levite of today are our White evangelical and, yes, our Black churches that are blind, deaf, and mute to the persistent oppression of African Americans.

While the Good Samaritan was taking care of the injured, who was going after the robbers? They must be stopped so they cannot hurt anyone else. God help the next victim if a Good Samaritan is not passing his way.

Would it surprise you to learn that Samaritan is termed "good" because of the racism embedded in the text? Samaritans were considered debauched and were not expected to do good. The Samaritan was an anomaly to his race. In truth, he is a son of God doing God's work. The indictment is with those who are numb to human suffering. Unfortunately, the church that once shined as the torch of hope for the marginalized has fallen into numbness past the point of no return. We have lost our ability to impact change. In the words of Jesus, "You are the salt of the earth. But if the salt loses its saltiness, how can it be made salty again? It is no longer good for anything, except to be thrown out and trampled underfoot" (Matthew 5:13).

Theological reflection not only invokes scriptures but tradition. This tradition might also employ negro spiritual, our ancestral heroes who fought, sacrificed, and gave their last breath for a better world. In the words of the prophet Amos, "But let justice roll on like a river, like a never-failing stream" (Amos 5:24).

Insertion grounds us in the suffering of our African Americans—in this case African American men. Social analysis looks for root and historical causes such as a history of enslavement, Jim Crow, institutional racism across every sector, and the intergenerational guardians of those systems. And, theological reflection gives us the impetus to disrupt and dismantle them. It brings Moses, and Joshua, Amos and Jeremiah, and Deborah and Rahab to the forefront so that they may remind us of how they fought for the liberation of their people. This conviction and connection with scripture was done with amazing poetry and force by MLK:

> We are not wrong, we are not wrong in what we are doing. If we are wrong, the Supreme Court of this nation is wrong. If we are wrong, the Constitution of the United States is wrong. And if we are wrong, God Almighty is wrong. If we are wrong, Jesus of Nazareth was merely a utopian dreamer that never came down to Earth. If we are wrong, justice is a lie, love has no meaning. And we are determined here in Montgomery to work and fight until "justice runs down like water, and righteousness like a mighty stream."[43]

This is theological reflection at its best.

Action—The Place Where Faith Meets Work

Preachers and clergy who complain about social and political problems diminish themselves and the offices that they hold when they fail to follow through with social action. When we speak without action, we become the loveless vessels that the Apostle Paul spoke about when he said,

"If I speak in the tongues of men or of angels, but do not have love, I am only a resounding gong or a clanging cymbal" (I Corinthians 13:1). Our love and our passion must drive us to do something. Many years ago, my wife and I took the Metro North to Manhattan to see the Christmas tree at Rockefeller Center. It was the first time we were taking our three young children to the city during the Christmas season. The evening was festive and cold. The train pulled into Grand Central Station where the lights and opulence dazzled the kids. They were attracted and distracted all at once by the beauty and busyness of the city. As we walked through marble tunnels to jump on the subway, we turned a corner and there, right in front of us on the cold concrete, was a homeless man sound asleep with a donation can in front of him. Admittedly, like all the other passersby, I had become numb to the homeless as a normative part of the landscape of New York City. Our five-year-old, Jonathon, grabbed my hand in horror and asked, "Daddy, why is he sleeping there on the floor?" My heart sank. With nine words, my five-year-old "unnumbed" me. He opened up my blinded eyes, as the song goes. He then cried, "Do something Daddy, *do something*!" And that's just it, isn't it? We must all do something to advance the cause for justice for Black men. Do something if you work in the school system. Do something if you work in the court system. Do something when you hear hate speech. Do something with your church budget that goes beyond your social celebration. Do something to advance justice for Black men and boys in the community.

The Rev. Bishop William J. Barber II is a kind of modern day prophet who travels the country forming partnerships with all sorts of institutions to combat poverty. His organization, The Poor People's Campaign: A National Call to Moral Revival, held a march in Washington, DC to bring awareness to the plight of the poor and disenfranchised.

> And when we do, we will know that we must act to reconstruct a society where everyone can thrive. Through stories and faces, tears, righteous videos, policy demands and data, this Poor People's Assembly and Moral March on Washington aims to expose the damage and deaths caused by interlocking injustices that do not have to exist. If Americans can see the reality of poverty, many will demand a response that shifts the moral narrative and changes the conversation about what is possible. Now is the time for a moral movement. The soul of our democracy depends on it.[44]

Local and regional church leaders must address the needs of those in their congregations and communities. To be more effective, churches must move beyond their sectarianism and become more collaborative in order to bolster their advocacy and impact.

Conclusion

The book of Acts is a call to be filled with the Spirit and bring justice to every corner of the world. "And you shall be witnesses to me both in Jerusalem, and in all Judaea, and in Samaria, and to the uttermost part of the earth" (Acts 1:8). It is an ever-expanding call to find justice for those who suffer—not because of misfortune but because of greed, White Supremacy, and the persistent legacy of slavery. The victims of racism and White supremacy, Black men are the most endangered of all groups in the United States. The White evangelical church has much work to do in facing themselves and much to answer for in how they have perpetuated oppression through their political ideology (like supporting Donald Trump's candidacy for president). They must finally acknowledge their White privilege and a gospel that turned Jesus into a White man who sides with power against the marginalized. Their missionary work is not enough. Their donations to earthquake and hurricane victims in Black and Brown countries are not enough. No, it's not enough to say that they have multiracial congregations. The work must begin with confronting bigotry, White supremacy, and a willingness to relinquish powers that render them better than me and my Black brothers.

On the other hand, the Black church must rediscover its prophetic fire. We must be reconverted. We must remember our rich and progressive history of confronting the racial injustice that Black men face in the United States and, indeed, around the world. We must do more. Like my son said, "Daddy, *do* something." That night, I did do something to help out that homeless man, but it was not enough. He needed a warm bed, possibly mental health support, reunification with his family, and a community which he could call his own. These are things that should be within our wheelhouse. But, we must go beyond the stopgap fillers. We must confront aggressive policing that leaves many of our young men dead or withering away behind bars. We must confront school systems that send children out into the world unable to read, write, or problem-solve. Indeed, we must confront attitudes that dub those on welfare, "welfare queens," and moochers but aspire to be rich like the corporate raiders. We must become the Jeremiah's of our time, crying:

My sadness and worry is making my stomach hurt.
I am bent over in pain.
I am so afraid.
My heart is pounding inside me.
I cannot keep quiet, because I have heard the trumpet blow.
The trumpet is calling the army to war.

Disaster follows disaster.
The whole country is destroyed.
Suddenly my tents are destroyed.
My curtains are torn down!
I hear the war trumpets?

Notes

1. W. Wilcox and N. Wolfinger, "How the Church Helps Black Men Flourish in America," The Atlantic 28 (2016).
2. Jeff Diamant, "Three-quarters of Black Americans Say Black Churches Have Helped Promote Racial Equality," Pew Research Center, https://policycommons.net/artifacts/1426335/three-quarters-of-black-americans-say-black-churches-have-helped-promote-racial-equality/2040751/.
3. Sharon E. Moore, A. Christson Adedoyin, Michael A. Robinson, and Daniel A. Boamah. "The Black Church: Responding to the Drug-Related Mass Incarceration of Young Black Males: 'If You Had Been Here My Brother Would Not Have Died!'" (2015).
4. Peter Block, *Community: The Structure of Belonging* (Berrett-Koehler Publishers, 2018.)
5. J. J. DiIulio, "Supporting Black Churches," *Brookings Review* 17, no. 2 (1999): 42–45.
6. Robert Joseph Taylor and Linda M. Chatters, "Church Members as a Source of Informal Social Support." *Review of Religious Research* (1988): 193–203.
7. Ibid.
8. William H. Becker, "The Black Church: Manhood and Mission." *Journal of the American Academy of Religion* 40, no. 3 (1972): 316–333.
9. Larry R. Morrison, "The Religious Defense of American Slavery before 1830." *Journal of Religious Thought* 37 (1980): 16–29.
10. James H. Cone, *The Cross and the Lynching Tree* (Orbis Books, 2011).
11. Henry Louis Gates Jr., *The Black Church: This Is Our Story, This Is Our Song* (Penguin, 2022).
12. James H. Cone, "Black Theology in American Religion," *Journal of the American Academy of Religion* 53 no. 4 (1985): 755–771.
13. Becker, William H. "The Black Church: Manhood and Mission," *Journal of the American Academy of Religion* 40, no. 3 (1972): 316–333.
14. Eddie Glaude Jr., "The Black Church Is Dead," *Huffington Post* 2, no. 24 (2010): 10.
15. Ibid.
16. Ibid.
17. Calvin B. Marshall III, "The Black Church—Its Mission Is Liberation," *The Black Scholar* 2, no. 4 (1970): 13–19.
18. Gary Dorrien, *The New Abolition: W. E. B. Du Bois and the Black Social Gospel* (Yale University Press, 2015).
19. James H. Cone, "Black Theology and the Black Church: Where do we go from here?" *Crosscurrents* 27, no. 2 (1977): 147–156.

20. Mark Chaves and Lynn M. Higgins, "Comparing the Community Involvement of Black and White Congregations," *Journal for the Scientific Study of Religion* (1992): 425–440.

21. Michael O. Emerson and Christian Smith, *Divided by Faith: Evangelical Religion and the Problem of Race in America* (Oxford University Press, 2001).

22. H. Mark Roelofs, "Liberation Theology: The Recovery of Biblical Radicalism," *American Political Science Review* 82, no. 2 (1988): 549–566.

23. Walter Brueggemann, *Prophetic Imagination*, revised edition (Fortress Press, 1978).

24. Sarah Travis, *Decolonizing Preaching: The Pulpit as Postcolonial Space*, vol. 6 (Wipf and Stock Publishers, 2014).

25. Anthea Butler, *White Evangelical Racism: The Politics of Morality in America* (UNC Press, 2021).

26. Randy S. Woodley and Bo C. Sanders, *Decolonizing Evangelicalism: An 11: 59 pm Conversation* (Wipf and Stock, 2020).

27. Matt Zapotosky, "Charleston Church Shooter: 'I Would Like to Make It Crystal Clear; I Do Not Regret What I Did,'" *Washington Post*, 2017.

28. Jean-Pierre Reed, "Christian Smith, Religion: What It Is, How It Works, and Why It Matters," (2020): 318–320.

29. Lenny Duncan, *Dear Church: A Love Letter from a Black Preacher to the Whitest Denomination in the US* (Fortress Press, 2019).

30. Frederick Douglass, *Frederick Douglass: Autobiographies (LOA# 68): Narrative of the Life/My Bondage and My Freedom/Life and Times*, Vol. 68. (Library of America, 1994).

31. Holland, Edward Joseph, and Peter J. Henriot. *Social analysis: Linking faith and justice.* (1984).

32. Bryan Stevenson, *Just Mercy (Movie Tie-In Edition): A Story of Justice and Redemption* (One World, 2019).

33. Edward Bell, "Graduating Black Males: A Generic Qualitative Study," *Qualitative Report* 19 (2014): 13.

34. John Fantuzzo, Whitney LeBoeuf, Heather Rouse, and Chin-Chih Chen, "Academic Achievement of African American Boys: A City-Wide, Community-Based Investigation of Risk and Resilience," *Journal of School Psychology* 50, no. 5 (2012): 559–579.

35. Sharon D. Jones-Eversley, Johnny Rice, A. Christson Adedoyin, and Lori James-Townes, "Premature Deaths of Young Black Males in the United States," *Journal of Black Studies* 51, no. 3 (2020): 251–272.

36. Vernon Brundage, "Labor Market Activity of Blacks in the United States," Division of Labor Force Statistics, US Bureau of Labor Statistics (2020).

37. Frank A. Sloan, Padmaja Ayyagari, Martin Salm, and Daniel Grossman, "The Longevity Gap between Black and White Men in the United States at the Beginning and End of the 20th Century," *American Journal of Public Health* 100, no. 2 (2010): 357–363.

38. Albert B. Cleage, *The Black Messiah* (Sheed and Ward, 1968); Earle J. Fisher, *The Reverend Albert Cleage Jr. and the Black Prophetic Tradition: A Reintroduction of the Black Messiah* (Rowman & Littlefield, 2021).

39. Dietrich Bonhoeffer, *Life Together: Prayerbook of the Bible*, vol. 5. (Fortress Press, 1995).

40. Sandra L. Barnes, "Black Church Culture and Community Action," *Social Forces* 84, no. 2 (2005): 967–994.

41. Martin Luther King Jr., "Letter from Birmingham Jail" (1964): 594–607.

42. Ali Vitali, Kasie Hunt, and Frank Thorp, "Trump Referred to Haiti and African Nations as 'Shithole' Countries," *NBC News* 3 (2018): 4–8.

43. Martin Luther King Jr., "Address to the First Montgomery Improvement Association (MIA) Mass Meeting," *A Call to Conscience: The Landmark Speeches of Dr. Martin Luther King, Jr.* (2013): 1–12.

44. Martha Wagonner, "Poverty Is This Country's 'Basic Moral Contradiction,' Bishop Barber Says during Founder's Day Speech at Chapman University," Poor People's Campaign, accessed August 28, 2022 from: https://www.poorpeoplescampaign.org/poverty-is-this-countrys-basic-moral-contradiction-bishop-barber-says-during-founders-day-speech-at-chapman-university

www.ingramcontent.com/pod-product-compliance
Lightning Source LLC
Chambersburg PA
CBHW050535270326
41926CB00015B/3243